THE HEARTLAND OF ASIA

DISCOVERY AND EXPLORATION

The Reader's Digest Association Limited, London

THE HEARTLAND OF ASIA

BY NATHALIE ETTINGER

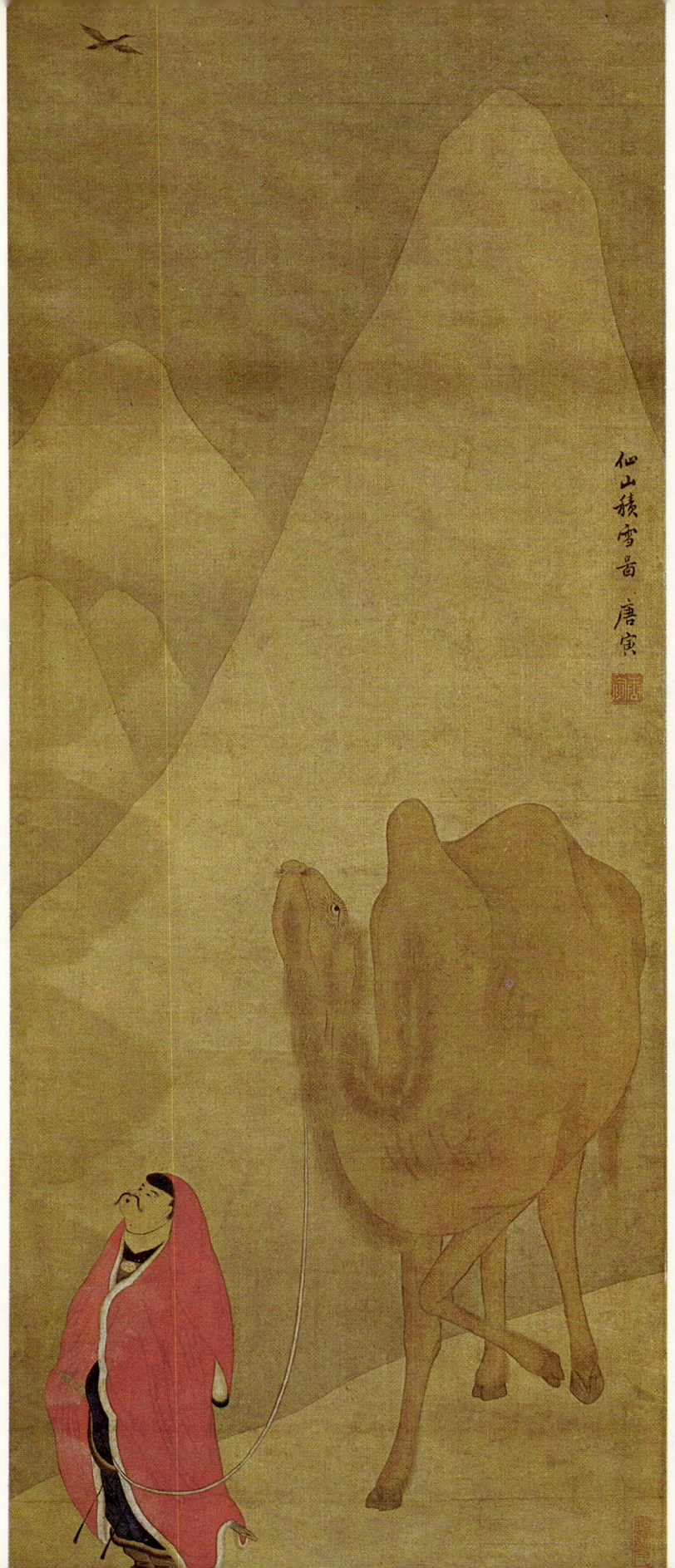

Executive Coordinators: Beppie Harrison
                        John Mason
Design Director: Guenther Radtke
Editorial: Ann Craig
           Damian Grint
           Gail Roberts
Picture Editor: Peter Cook
Research: Elizabeth Lake
Cartography by Geographical Projects

This edition published in the
United Kingdom and
Republic of Ireland by The
Reader's Digest Association Limited,
25 Berkeley Square, London, W1X 6AB
in association with
Aldus Books Limited, London
® READER'S DIGEST
is a registered trademark of The
Reader's Digest Association, Inc.
of Pleasantville, New York, U.S.A.

© 1971 Aldus Books Ltd, London
Reprinted with amendments 1980
First published in the United Kingdom
1971 by Aldus Books Ltd,
17 Conway Street, London, W.1.

Printed in Great Britain
by Hunt Barnard Web
Offset Ltd, Aylesbury

Contents

Left: a Chinese painting showing a man leading his camel through the mountains. These sturdy animals can travel hundreds of miles without food or water. They provided the early travelers across the Asian heartland with an invaluable method of transportation.

Frontispiece: a Persian miniature of a banquet, painted in about 1440. It was pictures like this that gave Europeans the idea that Asia was a land of colorful and gracious opulence.

List of Maps

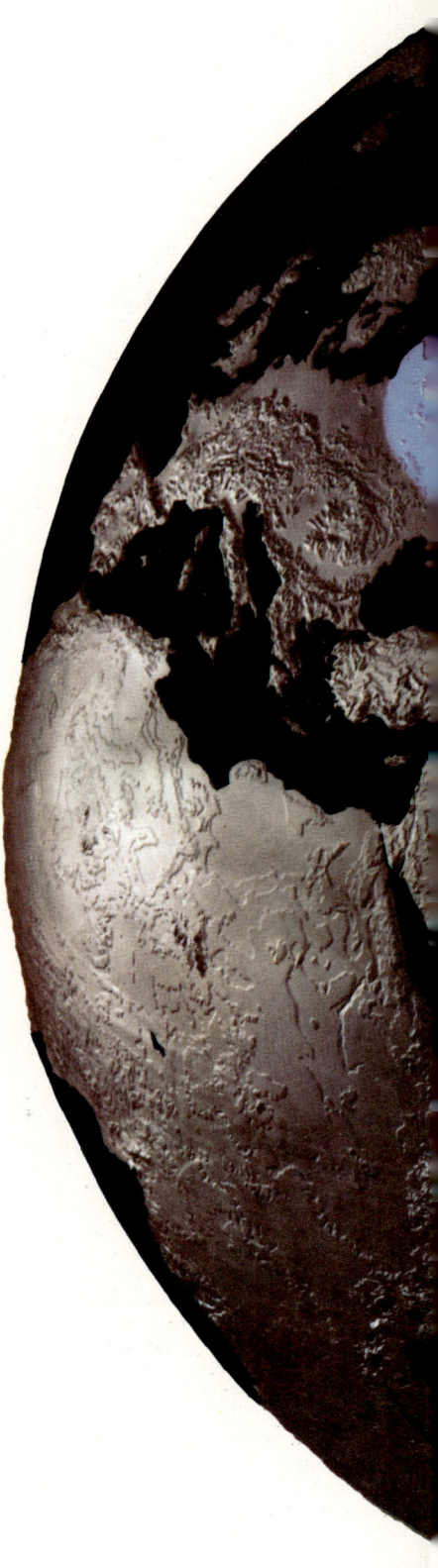

The illuminated globe highlights in blue the Asian heartland. At the beginning of the 1500's, Europeans knew little or nothing about this vast and forbidding region. By the early 1900's, however, many daring explorers had penetrated it, traveling by foot, or in caravans of camels and horses, deep into its most dangerous and hidden recesses.

Left: an engraving of the arms of the Company of Merchants of Russia, the Muscovy Company. This was formed during the reign of King Edward VI and legally incorporated during the reign of his elder sister, Mary.

Below: the plan of Moscow, as the city was when Chancellor saw it in the mid-1550's. At that time the buildings were made of wood, as shown in this plan, published in Cologne in 1572.

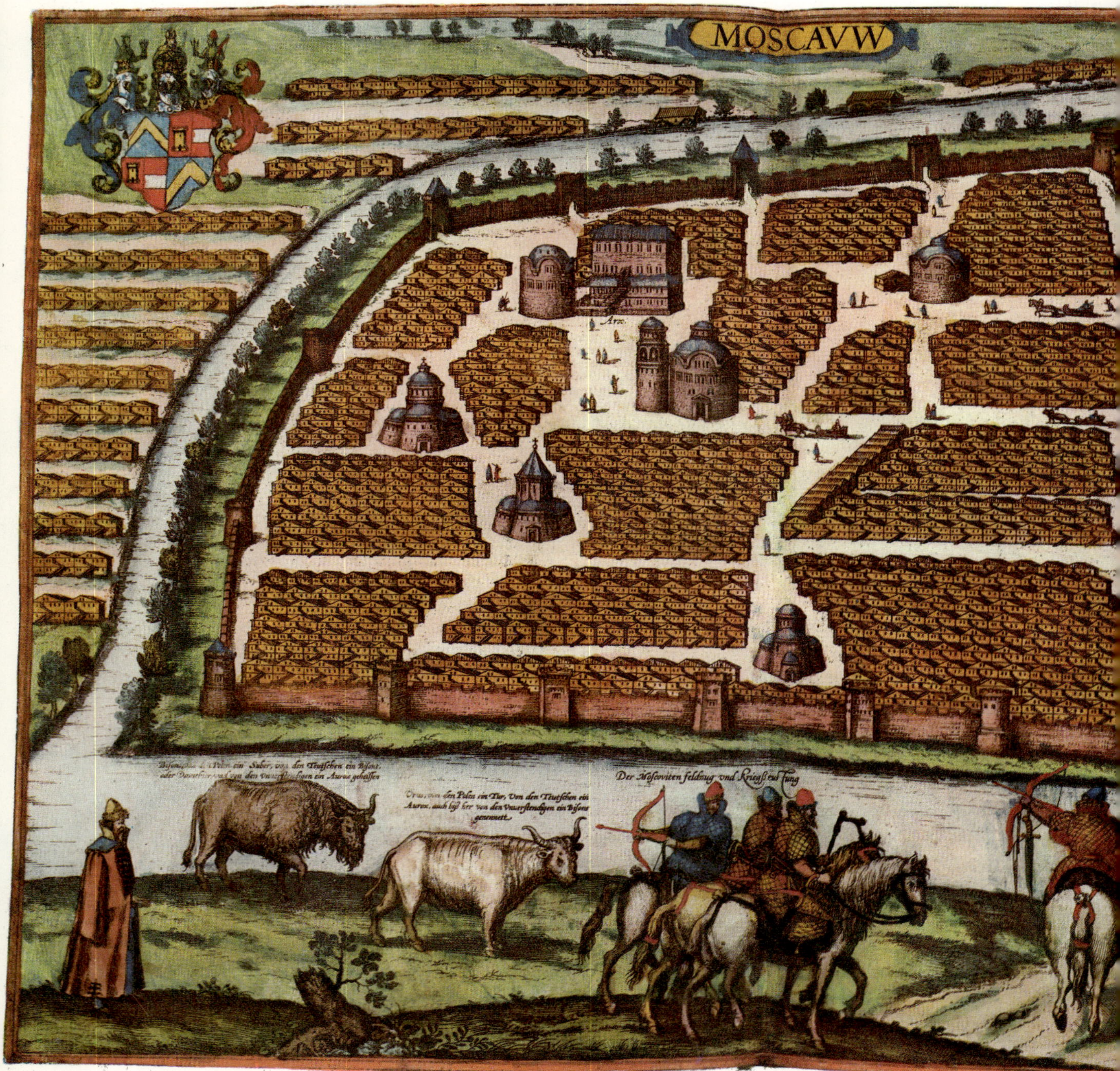

Northeast to Muscovy

1

MOSCOVIA, *vrbs, regionis eiusd̃ nominis metropolitica, duplo maior, quã Praga Boiemiæ, lignea ædificia habet, multas plateas, sed dispersas, latissimi campi interiacent: Mosca amnis, ipsam irrigat.*

On a bright May morning in 1553, an excited crowd began gathering at Greenwich, England, along the banks of the River Thames. All eyes were fixed on the fleet of ships just coming into view. In the vanguard was a throng of small boats rowed by men in sky-blue uniforms. Behind, at the end of stout towing ropes, were three tall-masted vessels, their rails and rigging alive with sailors. As the procession neared Greenwich Palace, the towing lines were cut, and the ships' sails were unfurled. Then all three vessels fired off a thunderous cannon salute. The crowd, now swelled by scores of courtiers from the palace, responded with wild enthusiasm, filling the air with shouts and cheers as the three ships gathered speed and moved off down the river to the sea.

It was a sendoff to make any mariner proud. But for Richard Chancellor, pilot-general of the fleet, it was less the cheers than the cries of "Farewell! Farewell! Godspeed!" that he remembered when the familiar shores of England had dropped out of sight. He was a widower, and had left behind two small sons. What would become of them, he wondered, if he should not come back? For this, he knew, would be no ordinary voyage. He and his commanding officer, Sir Hugh Willoughby, had been charged with the dangerous task of locating a Northeast Passage to the Orient. They were to sail through the cold, unknown waters beyond Norway, past the uppermost fringes of Asia, and then, hopefully, down the coast of Cathay (China) to the East Indies. No one knew what perils might lie along the way, let alone whether such a passage even existed.

Nevertheless, the hopes of many a man were pinned on the discovery of this Northeast Passage. The only other feasible route to the Orient—around the tip of Africa and through the Indian Ocean—had long been the exclusive monopoly of its discoverers, the Portuguese. Banned from using this vital seaway to the East, English merchants could neither compete for the spice trade nor find new markets for textiles, their own chief trading commodity. This was why the Northeast Passage held out such promise. At one and the same time, it would place the riches of the East within England's grasp, and open vital new outlets for England's manufactured goods.

The prime mover behind this search for the Northeast Passage was Sebastian Cabot, founder and governor of the Muscovy Company. Under his guidance, the Company had fitted out the three vessels

Above: portrait of a gentleman presumed to be Sebastian Cabot, by Lorenzo Lotto. He had made voyages to the New World for both England and Spain as a young man, and later became the founder of the Muscovy Company.

for the voyage, and procured the royal letters of introduction carried by Willoughby and Chancellor. These documents were addressed— with more hope than certainty—to "the Kings, Princes, and other Potentates inhabiting the Northeast partes of the worlde, toward the mighty Empire of Cathay."

On their departure, Willoughby and Chancellor had been instructed to keep the ships within sight of one another at all times. This they did until they reached the Lofoten Islands, high up along the coast of Norway. But there, meeting first with thick, swirling mists and

then with violent winds, they became separated. Chancellor later said that he became "very pensive, heavy and sorrowful" as he sailed on alone in the coming weeks. How much more depressed he might have been had he known that he would never see Willoughby again! Within the next few months, Willoughby and all his men were to freeze to death along the cold and barren coast of Lapland.

Chancellor continued northeast until he "came at last to the place where he found no night at all, but a continual light and brightness of the sun, shining clearly upon the huge and mighty sea."

Above: although Willoughby and Chancellor had instructions to remain together, they were separated by a wild storm along the coast of Norway. Such a furious storm is shown here, painted by Pieter Bruegel the Elder in about 1568, contemporary with the time of early voyages north to Russia.

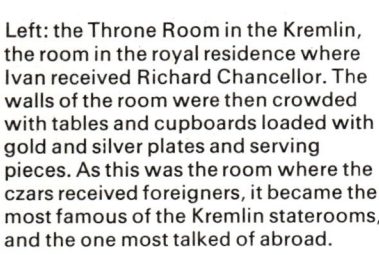

Well within the Arctic Circle, he rounded the northern tip of
Norway, where he found the coast curving southward, and soon
came to a large bay (the White Sea). There he sighted a settlement
and decided to land. When he stepped ashore, the inhabitants, awed
"by the strange greatness" of his ship, fell before him to kiss his
feet. Chancellor gently raised them up and asked to see their
governor. He came, and gave Chancellor to understand that the
village was Nenoska (near the present-day port of Archangel). The
governor added modestly that it was but a small outpost of the
great land of Muscovy, ruled by Czar Ivan IV.

At that time, few Englishmen had ever heard of Muscovy, or
Russia, as it later came to be called. Chancellor had found a new
route to Russia—and at a time when that nation was experiencing
the reign of its very first ruler to be crowned czar, the man whom
we call Ivan the Terrible.

Chancellor wanted to trade with the people of Nenoska, but they
were afraid to do so without the permission of Czar Ivan. When
Chancellor asked to see the czar, messengers were dispatched to the
court at Moscow. After waiting many days for a reply, Chancellor
determined to meet with the czar. Leaving most of his men behind,
he set out for Moscow, traveling overland in horse-drawn sledges
(heavy wooden sleighs), and escorted by strange men who wore fur

Right: an icon of the late 1400's or early 1500's, showing an important official of the Russian church, the Metropolitan Alexey. This was used as a holy image, and venerated in the same way as a similar icon of a saint or member of the Holy Family would be.

clothing and spoke a wild, incomprehensible language. It was a frightening journey, one that took them 700 miles over endless fields of snow and ice, through dark, brooding forests, and across gleaming frozen rivers.

When at long last the travelers reached their destination, Chancellor was immediately struck by the size—and the primitiveness—of the Russian capital. Though much larger than London, he wrote later, "It is very rude and standeth without all order." The houses were no more than log cabins, a fact that helped to account for the numerous blazing buildings Chancellor saw in the city during his stay. Most of the citizens seemed to be living in dire poverty, their cheerless existence relieved only by their constant tobacco smoking and heavy reliance on vodka. Chancellor was appalled by the number of drunken men and women he saw in the streets. More than once he saw the body of a person who had fallen down drunk in the snow and been left there to freeze to death or to be eaten by wild dogs.

The drabness of the citizen's dwellings contrasted strongly with the lavish residence of the czar. Situated in a walled sector of the city called the Kremlin, Ivan's gaudy palace did not at first impress the English sea captain, who remarked sarcastically that its exterior was "not of the neatest." But once through its portals, he was dazzled by its splendor. In the gilded throne room stood 100 courtiers, each dressed in golden robes. But by far the grandest figure in the court was the czar himself. Ivan's robes were heavily encrusted with precious stones, and the gems that glittered from his golden scepter fairly blinded Chancellor with their brilliance.

Awed by all this magnificence, the English captain hesitated a moment, then strode resolutely forward and presented the letter

Below: the capture of Kazan, Ivan's first major victory over the Mongols. This picture of the mid-1500's—Kazan fell in 1552—shows the conquest as a triumph of the Cross over the Crescent.

from his own king, Edward VI. Ivan received it gravely, then motioned his guest to join him at dinner. The banquet table was in keeping with the richness of the court. All the plates and goblets were made of gold, and every course, from the roast swans to the great tankards of mead, was presented with lavish ceremony.

Chancellor was royally entertained at the czar's expense for several weeks. During this time, he had ample opportunity to observe the Russian way of life, and many things struck him as strange. One of these was the Russians' Eastern Orthodox religion, an elaborate and traditional form of Christianity unknown in Western Europe. A Protestant himself, Chancellor saw in this unfamiliar religion "such an excess of superstition as the like hath not been heard of." He considered the Russians' veneration of *icons* (religious pictures) idolatrous, and found their church services utterly baffling. Repeatedly kneeling and mumbling the words "Oh Lord, have mercy upon us," the congregation seemed to "gaggle and duck like so many geese." But what most distressed Chancellor was the behavior of the priests. As far as he could tell, they were illiterate, overbearing, and as fond of vodka as the rest of the populace. Nevertheless, he noted, the Church was held in great respect, and seemed to possess at least a third of the nation's wealth.

But if Chancellor found the customs of the Church curious, he found the might of the czar positively awesome. Less than 100 years had elapsed since the country had shaken off the harsh rule of the ruthless "Golden Horde" of Mongol tribes that had swept down upon Muscovy in the 1200's. For two centuries, while Western Europe experienced the flowering of the Renaissance, generations of Muscovites had suffered under the cruel yoke of Mongol domination. Towns and cities had been burned to the ground, and many thousands slaughtered. The art of living had been lost in the struggle for survival. At last, in 1480, the grand prince of Moscow, Ivan III, had ceased to pay tribute to the Golden Horde. But by that time, the kingdom had fallen far behind Western Europe in the development of technology, statecraft, art, and scholarship.

The Mongols' single contribution to Russian civilization had been the lesson of tyranny. Ivan IV (the Terrible), grandson of Ivan III, had learned that lesson well. The first Russian ruler to be crowned czar, Ivan turned his attention to his grandfather's old enemies, the Mongols, driving them out of Astrakhan, their stronghold on the Caspian Sea, and extending Russia's borders southward to the lower Volga River basin. After the defeat of the Mongols, Ivan turned his attention to reducing any threat to his power that might come from inside the country. He created a small army of secret police and began a reign of terror, reducing the power of the country's nobility by having hundreds of aristocrats arrested and executed. He put whole towns and villages to the sword, and murdered any church officials who opposed him. He initiated laws that bound the peasants more closely to the land, and this was a major step in the establishment of serfdom.

Right: the busy port of Hamburg in the late 1400's. Since the early 1100's, enterprising merchants from a group of north German cities known as the Hanseatic League had held a near-monopoly of trade in the Baltic, and in particular with Russia. Hamburg was one of the most important of these Hanseatic towns. Here Russian grain, honey, and furs were exchanged for European metal work and linens.

The basis of Ivan's power lay in his absolute control over the immense Russian army. Made up of men who had nothing else in the world but what he chose to give them, it was a force to be reckoned with. Chancellor was deeply impressed by the iron discipline and physical stamina of the soldiers: "They are a kind of people most sparing in diet and most patient in extremity of cold," he wrote. "For when the ground is covered with snow and is grown terrible and hard with the frost, this Russ hangs up his mantle, or soldier's coat, against that part whence the wind and snow drives, and so, making a little fire, lies down with his back toward the weather; his drink is cold water from the river, mingled with oatmeal, and this is all his good cheer."

While Chancellor was busy admiring Russia's army and criticizing its religion, he was also engaged in appraising its trading possibilities. He had already found buyers for the woolen goods he had brought with him, and had taken a shrewd look at what the Russians had to offer in exchange. It was an impressive list: flax, hemp, wax, honey, salt, oil, and—most valuable of all—furs. Among these were fox, beaver, and seal, as well as luxurious mink, ermine, and sable.

But if Chancellor was delighted with the prospect of trade with Russia, Ivan was equally delighted with the prospect of ties with England. Anxious to pursue his wars against the Mongols, he was eager for powerful Western allies, and even more eager for the military supplies he knew England could provide. Thus, when Chancellor returned to England in 1554, he carried with him a warmly welcoming letter from the czar, promising England the most generous trading terms and privileges if her merchants would do him the honor of visiting his country.

Mary Tudor, who had become Queen of England during Chancellor's absence, was well pleased with the outcome of his voyage. She at once granted the Muscovy Company a special charter and urged them to waste no time in sending traders to Russia. For the moment, the grand scheme of opening up a Northeast Passage was laid aside. In reaching Russia, Chancellor had located a vastly promising new market, one that was not only nearer than Cathay, but one that had the potential of becoming an English monopoly.

Thus began a lively commercial romance between England and her new-found trading partner. The very next year, Richard

Left: Antony Jenkinson, shown in an Elizabethan miniature by Nicholas Hilliard in 1588. He was a young man, already very experienced in foreign travel, when he was chosen to take the place of Chancellor, who had drowned.

Right: a Russian church—the Church of the Intercession of the Virgin—in winter. In Jenkinson's time, and for years afterward, travel in Russia was only really easy during the winter, when the surfaces of roads and fields had frozen hard. During the summer almost all travel was stopped by mud.

Chancellor made a second voyage to Russia. Again he had no trouble selling his wares, and again he was royally entertained in Moscow. And this time, Chancellor obtained from the czar an official document granting the Muscovy Company the right to buy and sell wherever they liked in the czar's domains. But the brave captain did not live to carry the good news back to England himself. On the return voyage, his ship ran into a storm off the coast of Scotland, and Chancellor, along with many of his men, was drowned.

The man chosen to take Chancellor's place as merchant-ambassador to Russia was Antony Jenkinson, an experienced traveler who had already journeyed far and wide through Europe, Asia Minor, and northern Africa. Like Chancellor before him, Jenkinson was to serve as an agent for the Muscovy Company to the court of the czar.

Some time after reaching Russia in the summer of 1557, Jenkinson set out for Moscow, traveling first by boat and later by horse-drawn sledges. By changing the horses every 40 miles, the travelers made rapid progress, gliding over the endless Russian plains in an eerie silence broken only by the tinkle of the harness bells. As they swept along, the runners of the sledges left a shimmering trail in the snow beneath the branches of bare, frost-covered birch trees that looked, as a later traveler put it, "like white coral encrusted with brilliant diamond dust."

Jenkinson arrived in Moscow just in time to attend the czar's lavish Christmas banquet, and a few days later he was invited to witness the Twelfth Night "Blessing of the Waters." This ceremony began with a long procession from the largest church in the city to the Moskva River. At the head marched the Church officials carrying icons and a large wooden cross. Behind them walked the czar, accompanied by all his *boyars* (high-ranking landowners). The candlelit procession slowly wound its way through the city streets and down to the river, where a great hole had been hacked in the ice. Before a hushed crown, the *patriarch* (chief bishop of the Church)

Above: an engraving of the late 1600's showing the Blessing of the Waters on the Twelfth Night of Christmas. Antony Jenkinson witnessed this annual ceremony when he visited Russia in 1558.

formally blessed the water, then sprinkled some of it on the czar and the boyars. "This done," reports Jenkinson, "divers children were thrown in, and sick people, and plucked out quickly again, and divers Tartars christened."

Jenkinson later learned that this type of enforced baptism was considered the surest—and the quickest—way to convert the heathen. It was common practice to drive newly conquered Mongols, fleeing for their lives, into the nearest river. Then, as they crawled back to shore, more dead than alive, a Russian priest standing on the bank would make the sign of the cross over them, officially turning them into Christians.

Instant conversion was not the only tradition Jenkinson took note of during his stay in Russia. He observed the country's marriage customs closely and found them "in most points abominable." He reports that, "One common rule is amongst them, that if the woman be not beaten with the whip at least once a week she will not be good, and the women say that if their husbands did not beat them they would not love them." Indeed, a Russian wife's position was exceedingly precarious at the best of times. If a man wished to marry

Left: by the time Jenkinson returned to England, Elizabeth I was on the throne. This portrait, by an unknown artist in 1560, shows her dressed for her coronation on January 15, 1559.

again, he simply disposed of the wife he already had by driving her into a nunnery or flogging her to death—a form of "correction" not punishable by law.

In April, 1558, Jenkinson received the czar's permission to travel south to Astrakhan. Because roving bandits made travel through the countryside hazardous, he made the journey by boat down the Volga River with an armed escort. When the party reached the lower Volga River Basin, Jenkinson had his first encounter with the Mongols. He was shocked by their primitive way of life. A nomadic people, they moved from place to place on horseback, and scorned the growing of crops. They said that it was the practice of eating bread, "made from the top of a weed [wheat]" that made the Christians so weak. They themselves lived on a diet of horsemeat, often eaten raw (the original form of modern-day "steak Tartare"), and on fermented mare's milk.

But the Mongols Jenkinson saw in Astrakhan were far from flourishing. Only two years had passed since Ivan's army had conquered the region, and the effects of the war were still being felt. Astrakhan was in the grip of famine and plague, and heaps of decaying bodies lay everywhere. Over 100,000 had died, and the miserable survivors were being sold as slaves. Jenkinson reports that he could have bought any number of Mongol children for the price of a single loaf of bread.

The Englishman's journey did not end at Astrakhan. Hoping to reach Cathay, he sailed across the Caspian Sea and traveled eastward by caravan to the Mongol *khanate* (princedom) of Bukhara. But there, 800 miles from the Caspian, fierce tribal fighting turned him back. Disappointed, he returned to Moscow, paid his respects to the czar, and set sail for England. He found the nation rejoicing over the recent accession of young Queen Elizabeth I. Like Queen Mary before her, Elizabeth heartily approved of the Muscovy Company's activities. And so it was with her blessing, in 1566, that Antony Jenkinson was again sent to Moscow. This time, his task was to negotiate for an exclusive English trading monopoly in Russia.

Jenkinson's mission was completely successful. Not only did the czar grant the wished-for monopoly, he also promised that merchants from any other country would have their goods confiscated. But Ivan wanted something in exchange. He was beginning to feel more and more menaced by his enemies, and, in 1567, Queen Elizabeth received a secret letter from him asking if she would grant him asylum in England if he were forced to flee. He also requested England's help in his wars against Poland. The queen was quite willing to give asylum to the czar, but she was not prepared to involve her country in a military alliance with him.

After an exchange of high ranking ambassadors and lengthy negotiations, it became obvious to Ivan that Elizabeth would not consent to his proposed alliance. In retaliation he took away every trading privilege he had thus far granted to the Muscovy Company. It took a special mission to the czar by Jenkinson in 1571 to heal the breach and recoup the Company's trading privileges in Russia.

In spite of Jenkinson's success, the next 12 years were marked by uncertain relations between Russia and England. In order to again press his case for an alliance with England, Ivan requested an exchange of ambassadors. Elizabeth's choice for the position in Moscow was Sir Jerome Bowes, whose boldness and bravado in the presence of the czar gave rise to a whole host of exaggerated anecdotes about him.

For instance, it was said that Bowes, on his very first meeting with Ivan, refused to doff his hat. Outraged, Ivan roared that the only other man who had ever refused to do so had been punished by having his hat nailed to his head. Bowes still would not comply, explaining that he was "the ambassador of the invincible Queen of England, who does not veil her bonnet nor bare her head to any Prince living." Ivan was impressed with this display of courage and loyalty. "Look you there!" he said to his boyars, "There is a brave fellow indeed that dares to do and say this much for his mistress," and thereupon gave Bowes a hearty welcome.

Bowes was the last English ambassador to the court of Moscow

Right: both England and Russia were eager to establish trade, with Russia desiring the fine English wool as much as the English wanted Russian furs. Here a table carpet of the 1500's is decorated in part with a scene of shepherds and their flocks, the raw materials of the important wool trade.

Below: this carved bench-end, also from the 1500's, shows an English cloth-weaver of the time, apparently at work pressing a piece of cloth.

before the death of Ivan. The czar had been slowly going mad, and this had resulted in a long series of cruel persecutions and arbitrary executions.

The death of Ivan in 1584 failed to bring stability to Russia. Instead, the country was plunged into an era of bloody civil war and dynastic intrigue. This period, known as the "Time of Troubles", ended in 1613, with the accession of Czar Michael Romanov. The Romanovs were to rule Russia for the next 300 years, until the Bolshevik Revolution of 1917 ended the empire.

Right: the reception of the foreign ambassadors by the Czar Alexis, as shown in Adam Olearius's account of his visits to Moscow, published in 1647. In the ceremonial chamber the boyars and court officials served mainly as decorative background.

Left: Sir Jerome Bowes, wearing his hat. His stubborn insistence on his queen's dignity—and his own, as her representative—won Ivan's respect.

It was during Czar Michael's reign that intercourse with Western Europe was revitalized. Among the travelers were men from countries other than England, for by now, Russia was actively seeking trade with a variety of nations. One of these was the tiny German state of Holstein, which sent embassies to Moscow in 1634, 1636, 1639, and 1643. All four missions included a man named Adam Olearius, whose special duty it was to gather useful information about Russian customs.

Olearius was a keen observer, and wrote vividly about his experiences in Russia. He records that shortly after his arrival in 1634, while riding through one of the villages in the north of the empire, his party was suddenly set upon by swarms of bees. "The horses began to wince, stand upon their hinder feet, and beat the ground as if they were bewitched"—much to the alarm of their riders. Olearius later learned that "it was a strategem of the inhabitants, who had incensed the bees purposely to prevent our lodging in the village."

In his report, Olearius describes Russian men as "corpulent, fat and strong, and of the same color as other Europeans." About the women he says that they "are well-proportioned, having passable good faces, but they paint so palpable [i.e., use such heavy make-up], that if they had a handful of meal cast in their faces, they could not disfigure themselves as much as the paint does."

As in Chancellor's time, there were frequent fires in Moscow. A good many of them were caused by the carelessness of tobacco smokers, and during Olearius' first visit to Muscovy, a special proclamation was issued forbidding the smoking of tobacco. Perhaps it was this deprivation that made the Russians Olearius saw so irritable. They were, he concluded, "a very quarrelsome people, who assail each other like dogs, with fierce, harsh words."

But the aspect of Russian life that most impressed Olearius was its extreme insularity. He records that the people were forbidden to travel abroad on pain of death, in order that "they might stay tranquil in slavery and not see the free institutions that exist in foreign lands." This was one reason why there was so little interest in learning or scholarship inside the empire. As Olearius puts it, "Just as they are ignorant of the praiseworthy sciences, they are little interested in memorable events or the history of their fathers, and they care little to find out the qualities of foreign peoples."

In fact, even the learning of a foreign language was officially banned in Russia at this time, and all foreign visitors were regarded with dark suspicion. Baron Augustine Meyerberg, the Austrian ambassador to Moscow from 1661 to 1663, voiced a familiar complaint when he said that the Russians made no distinction between peaceful diplomats and prisoners of war. Meyerberg himself was kept under virtual house arrest during the whole of his stay in Moscow.

But suspicion of foreigners and foreign ideas did not prevent the Russians from employing Western technicians to perform the tasks their own lack of learning rendered impossible. One such foreign expert was Samuel Collins, an English doctor who, in 1660, traveled to Moscow to become the czar's private physician. Collins spent nine years in Russia, and seems to have been well enough content there, despite the drawbacks of living in a society where "the people . . . look upon Learning as a Monster, and fear it no less than a Ship of Wildfire."

Certainly the good doctor found Russian justice no match for England's due process of law. As he wrote later, "Their judiciary proceedings are very confused. The accused cannot be condemned although a thousand witnesses come in against him, except he confesses the fact; and to this end they want not torments to extort confessions." The punishment meted out to those found plotting against the state was harsh in the extreme. "Traitors are severely tormented and afterward sent to Siberia, and [along] the way . . . softly put under the ice."

To us today, the very word "Siberia" has a forlorn ring to it, reminding us of the countless political prisoners who have died in its grim labor camps. But in Dr. Collins' day, there were as yet no official Siberian prison camps, and "Sibir," as it is called in Russian, generally had other, more hopeful connotations. To the majority of Russians, it was still "a vast, unknown province, reaching to the walls of Cathay," a frontier land as rich in potential as it was rife with danger.

As early as the 1570's a Dutch merchant named Oliver Brunel had penetrated this harsh and mysterious land in the unfulfilled hope of reaching Cathay. However, the savage land that lay beyond the Urals was not to be tamed by mere merchants from the West. The conquest of the vast Siberia called for men as uncompromising as the land itself.

Above: one of the engravings made from sketches by Baron Augustine Meyerberg. During his time in Russia he made many drawings of the ambassadorial precinct in Moscow, where he complained that he was treated much like a prisoner of war.

Right: the trade between Russia and England continued fitfully—these English knives, dated 1607, were brought back to England from Russia where they were found in the 1800's. They carry the London Cutler's Company proof mark, and have carved ivory handles representing English monarchs.

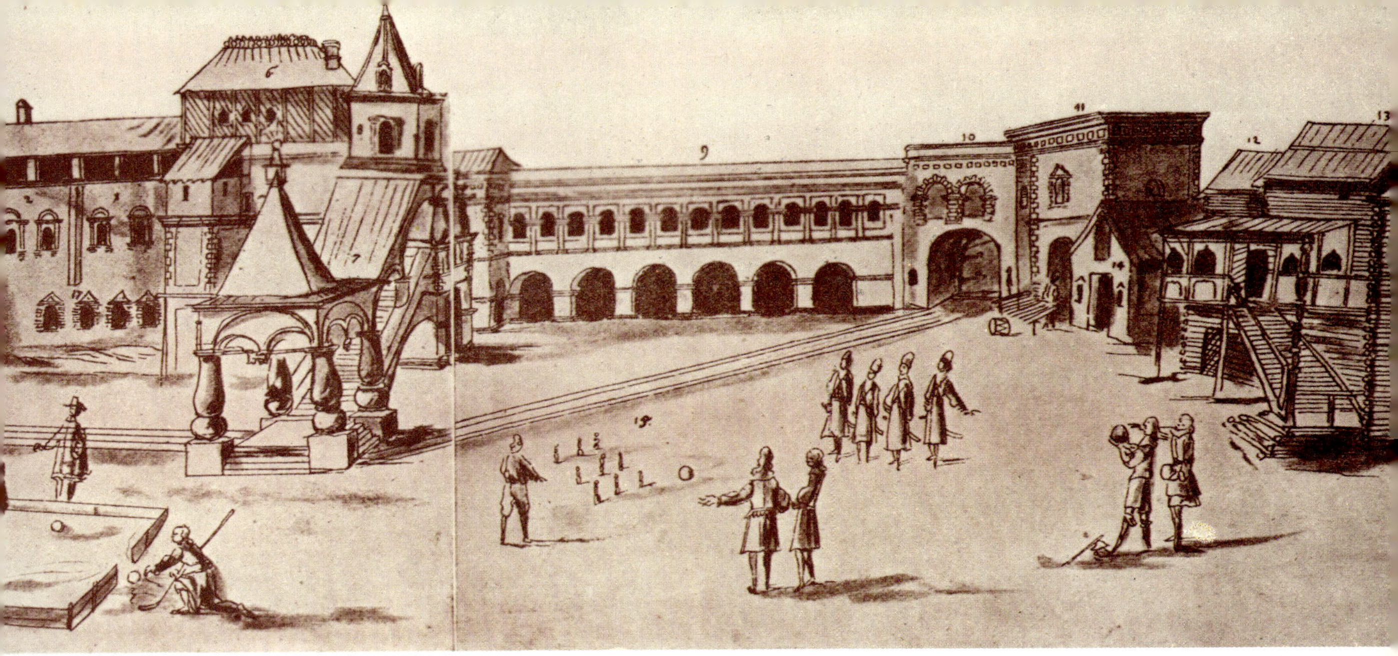

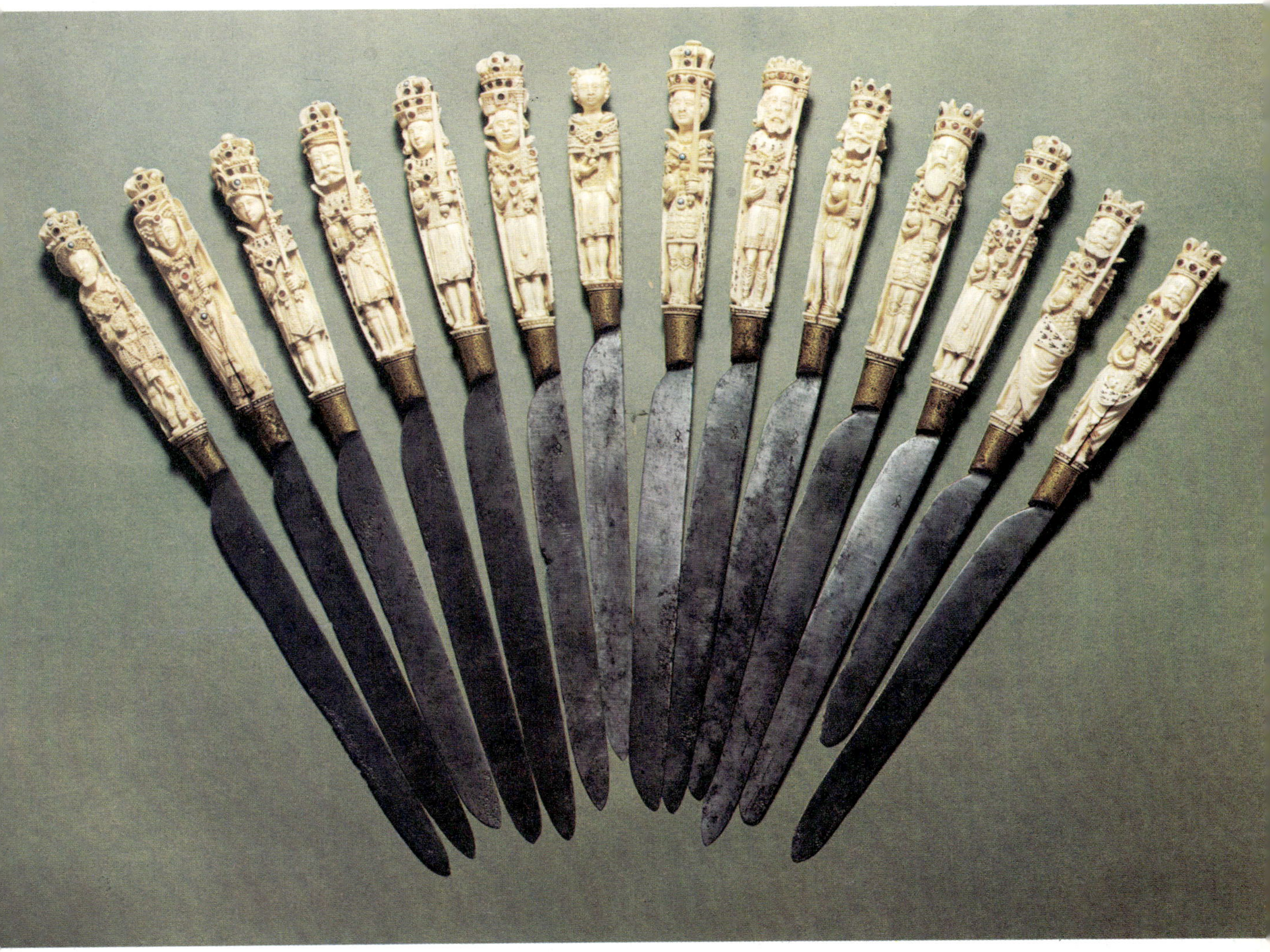

Below: Siberia, from a world map of
1550 by Pierre Desceliers. The topo-
graphy is almost entirely imaginary,
populated by strange monsters. In
the center is the Mongol Khan.

The Siberian Frontier

2

However bleak and desolate northern Russia had appeared to English visitors in the mid-1500's, it was, in fact, a travelers' paradise compared to Siberia. Russia, after all, was an established kingdom with established frontiers. Within its confines, no traveler could journey far without finding a town or village where he might stop to warm up and ask directions. In fact, despite its newness to the English, Russia was really a "known" land, even a tamed land.

Not so Siberia; in the 1550's, this northern third of Asia loomed almost as mysterious as the dark side of the moon. Few Western Europeans had ever been as far as the Ural Mountains, where Siberia begins, let alone into the 4 million square miles of *tundra* (flat, treeless plains), marshland, forest and *steppe* (grassland) beyond. How far east would a man have to travel through these trackless wastes to reach Cathay? What manner of strange people and places might he see along the way? Only a few adventurous Russian merchants knew the answers to these questions—and for good reason. Siberia—and, indeed, all of Central Asia—was still in the viselike grip of the Mongols, and few men were willing to risk an unnecessary encounter with them. Siberia might have remained a mysterious and forbidding land had it not been for one of those curious tricks of history that matches the right man to the right challenge at the right time.

The story begins in the 1550's, when a family of Russian merchants named Stroganov established a series of trading posts in the western foothills of the Ural Mountains. Finding that the Samoyeds, a nomadic tribe of northern Siberia, would accept mere trinkets for their ermines and sables, the Stroganovs established a brisk trade with the tribe and soon became very wealthy. To speed delivery of the pelts, the Stroganovs built trading posts farther and farther east until, by 1574, they were poised to break through the Ural Mountains and establish posts in Siberia itself. Their business expansion was, however, faced with a deadly check—the powerful *Khanate* of Sibir, which was ruled by Kutchum Khan.

Maxim Stroganov, head of the Ural trading station, was about to close the post and go home, when an extraordinary collection of men arrived at his camp. He counted almost 800 of them, weary and bedraggled, and obviously on the run. He had no need to ask who they were. It was clear that they were Cossacks, fleeing from the armies of the czar.

The sight of Cossacks on the move was not unusual in Muscovy.

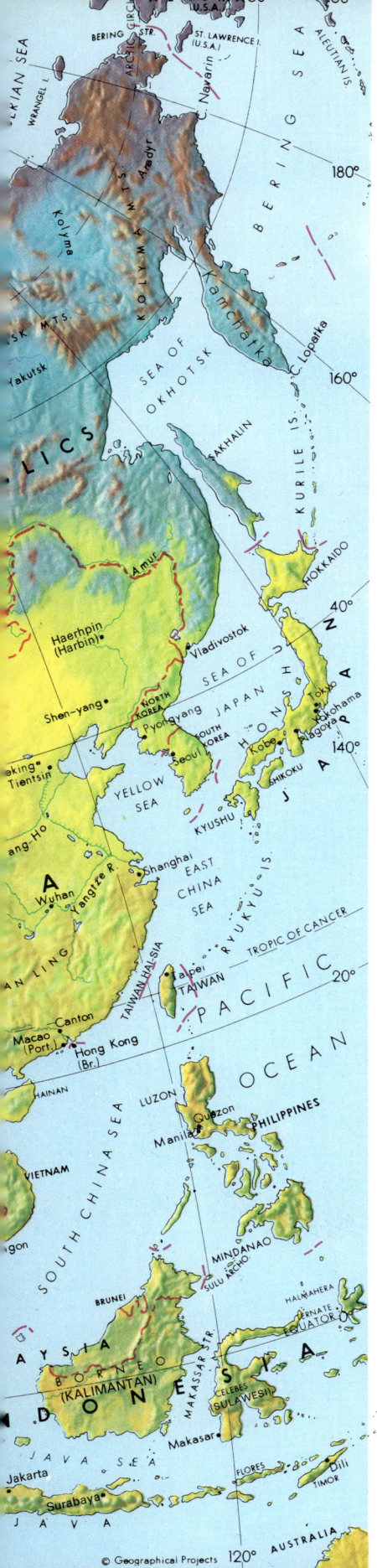

Left: Eurasia. Northern Asia's sprawling deserts, frozen wastes, and lofty mountain ranges make it one of the most bleak and challenging regions in the world.

These "free laborers," or "freebooters," as some would have it, were a law unto themselves, a rebel army of hard-riding brigands who roamed at will throughout Russia. Their forefathers, runaway serfs and outlaws from southwestern Russia and eastern Poland, had banded together early in the 1400's to form their own fugitive society. Always ready to give refuge to people in trouble, they had soon been joined by many other brave and desperate men and, by the mid-1500's, were numbered in the thousands.

Restless and venturesome, most Cossacks considered farming a foolish waste of time, and possessed few permanent villages. Most of them preferred the proud, free life of the wayfarer, moving swiftly over the southern steppes on horseback, or scudding down the rivers in the streamlined sailboats they called "seagulls." They lived by piracy, swooping down on towns, estates, and rich monasteries to loot and plunder. They were feared far and wide and, as a Turkish chronicler later wrote, "It can be stated with confidence that one cannot find bolder men on earth who care less about life . . . and fear death less." But if, as another writer put it, a Cossack's life was "rough, tough, short, and cheap," it was also vivid and joyful. They loved to dance, drink, and make merry, and were known everywhere for their haunting folk songs, which seemed to echo the wild and lonely beauty of their beloved steppes.

From time to time, the Cossacks hired themselves out to the czars as mercenary soldiers—but only on condition that they be allowed to keep their independence. They fought the Mongols in Astrakhan for Ivan the Terrible, and played a vital role in the region's conquest. But the Cossacks' triumphs in Astrakhan did not make up for the havoc they continued to wreak in Russia. Ivan was prepared to let them rule themselves, but not to let them terrorize the country. When the town of Nogoy was sacked and burned early in 1577, the czar dispatched an army to find and destroy the Cossacks responsible.

These were the hunted men who arrived at Maxim Stroganov's camp in the summer of 1577. Their leader, a fierce-looking man named Yermak, approached Stroganov and asked for employment for himself and his men. To the Russian trader, it seemed a heaven-sent opportunity. Who *but* the Cossacks could drive the Mongols out of Western Siberia? Stroganov offered Yermak and his followers a supply of new muskets if they would take on the Mongols

33

beyond the mountains. The assignment was a daunting one, but Yermak did not hesitate to accept it. Behind, in Russia, were the dogged armies of the czar and almost certain capture. Ahead, in Siberia, were the Mongol barbarians and the possibility of a splendid conquest. It was a challenge no Cossack could resist.

In early 1580, Yermak led his men across the Ural Mountains, built a fleet of boats, and then sailed down the Tura River into western Siberia. There, after a brief skirmish with a small band of Mongols, the Cossacks built a camp in which to wait out the winter. The cold was intense, often reaching temperatures of −40°F., and

Above: the Cossacks were traditionally scornful of authority from any quarter. Here, in an incident well known in Russian folklore, Cossacks compose a mocking letter to a sultan who had dared to offer them his protection.

Left: two Cossacks of the Caucasus, in a watercolor by Sir Robert Ker Porter. By the early 1800's, when this picture was painted, it was common for Cossack soldiers to make up special regiments in the czar's armies.

sometimes a man keeping the night watch would freeze to death in his tracks. But the Cossacks were a tough breed, and when they broke camp and set off again the following spring, there were very few gaps in the ranks.

Again they followed the Tura, moving swiftly down the river in their streamlined "seagulls." News of their prowess in battle had already reached the local Mongol ruler, Kutchum Khan, via the Mongol forces Yermak had routed the previous year. Kutchum had heard the Cossacks described as "invincible warriors in winged boats, with fiery unseen arrows [bullets] and death-bearing thunder." Determined to stop their advance, the khan prepared an ingenious ambush. He had heavy chains stretched across the Tobol River, and stationed hundreds of bowmen along the banks. In due course, the boats were sighted coming down the river, and the assembled Mongols, facing upstream, prepared to rain a hail of arrows on the figures they could see crowding the gunwhales. Too late, they saw that the "men" in the boats were merely bundles of straw dressed in Cossack shirts! The real Cossacks had come around by land, and were already shooting and cutting their way through the Mongol ranks from behind.

Driving their fleeing enemies before them, Yermak and his men struck out for Sibir, Kutchum Khan's capital on the banks of the Irtysh River. There the khan had assembled a mighty army, many times the size of Yermak's. But the Cossacks possessed two advantages over their enemies: superior military strategy, and a fierce determination to win against all odds. These qualities won the day for them, and, on November 7, 1581, Yermak marched triumphantly into Sibir.

But the conquest of the Mongol capital did not mean the end of Mongol resistance. Garrisoned at Sibir, the Cossacks were surrounded by a countryside still in arms. More serious, Yermak had by now lost almost 500 of his men—the victims of disease and

Below: Samoyeds at the temporary market at Obdorsk. The Samoyed people were determinedly nomadic, and after some clashes with the Russians came to the agreement that they would hold a yearly market and sell their furs, but only on the condition that the Russians would build no permanent structure on Samoyed land. The market was held on the border, in February, so it was always dark. This picture shows the scene, with a Russian church in the background to indicate the sovereignty of Russia.

starvation, as well as of battle. Reinforcements were desperately needed. In 1582, Yermak sent a messenger to Moscow to lay the newly conquered realm at the czar's feet and beg for assistance in its defense.

Ivan's response to this astonishing news was instantaneous. At once he showed approval of Yermak's Siberian conquest by granting him a full pardon for all his past crimes. In token of his gratitude, he sent the Cossack leader his own royal mantle. Lastly, he acknowledged Yermak as his special representative in Siberia and informed him that 500 of his best soldiers were on their way.

The fresh troops and supplies were not, however, sufficient. Yermak and some of his men were ambushed near Sibir and, in trying to make his escape, Yermak was drowned in the mighty Irtysh River. After the death of their leader, the last 150 Cossacks immediately left Siberia, but only to return again with reinforcements. With their help, the Cossacks built a new fortress at Tobolsk, 12 miles from Sibir, and began to extend their power eastward.

They soon reached the Ob River, which runs through the center of the West Siberian Plain. Moving north on the Ob, they met the Samoyed tribes, which populate much of northern Siberia. The

Above: the battle between the Mongols and Yermak's men on the banks of the Irtysh River. In the background is the Mongol stronghold of Isker, one of the many places captured by Yermak and his hard-riding Cossack forces.

Cossacks thought them a strange people because they used reindeer instead of horses, and followed a primitive religion that called for the bloody sacrifice of animals on crude altars of stone. Nonetheless, the Samoyeds seemed to be friendly and well intentioned. They were anxious to please their Cossack visitors with gifts and demonstrations of magic, and anxious, too, to begin trading with the Russians again.

But the Samoyeds' usefulness as middlemen in the Siberian fur trade was past. Now that the Cossacks had forged a way into western Siberia, the Russians themselves could procure the ermines and sables that fetched such a handsome price back in Moscow. Russian traders were soon beating a path eastward over the Ural Mountains, and the traffic in furs grew so rapidly that, by 1600, more than a million pelts were pouring into Moscow from the Siberian outposts every year.

But the real exploration and conquest of this harsh new land remained in the hands of the Cossacks. Seeking excitement and adventure, they came by the hundreds, lured on by the sheer expanse of a territory that seemed to stretch away to the very edge of the world. There, in a realm of wolves and bears, blizzards and dust storms, lay a challenge formidable enough to test the bravest man. And many brave men died in taking up that challenge. On one occasion, a party of 129 Cossacks, caught by the sudden onset of winter, were forced to make camp on an icy marshland deep in the wilderness. Many soon starved to death. Driven mad by hunger, the others ate their dead companions, then took to killing one another for food. By spring, there were only 30 survivors. These stark facts speak tellingly of the grim choices to be made in a land where nature itself is savage and uncompromising.

By the early 1600's, the majority of the Mongols had drifted southward, but there were still scattered tribes ready to offer resistance as the Cossacks swept eastward to the Yenisey River, and thence over the Central Siberian Plateau to the Lena River and Lake

Below: an engraving showing a Russian embassy at Regensburg in 1576. At this time, embassies were actually trade missions. Behind the ambassador come the boyars carrying furs, the staple of Russia's foreign trade.

Right: a wooden fort at Bratsk, on the Angara River. The fort was built in 1631 as a collecting center for furs for the czars. Originally the men who took the furs for the czar were soldiers, some of them Yermak's surviving Cossacks, but later, other hunted men—runaways from central Russia and Cossacks from the Don River area—came to try their luck in the vast expanses of the Siberian forests.

Baykal. There, along the shores of the deepest lake in the world, they encountered tribes like the Tungus and Buriats—nomadic hunters and herdsmen who lived in caves and used primitive stone tools. More often than not, these tribes proved hostile, and the Cossacks frequently had to fight a series of pitched battles before they could move on.

In the wake of the Cossacks came the ever-eager fur traders, and behind them, government officials sent by the czar to collect tribute from conquered tribes. Lastly came a few brave settlers who saw the vast Siberian grazing lands as a place to build farms and villages. Market towns were established farther and farther east: Tomsk, on the Tom River in 1604; Krasnoyarsk on the Yenisey River in 1628; and Yakutsk, on the Lena River in 1632.

But always it was the Cossacks who led the way. In 1638, they began pioneering a route eastward from Yakutsk through the East Siberian Uplands. After many months of toiling through rough and rocky terrain, they found the land sloping away abruptly toward a vast body of water—the Sea of Okhotsk. There, nearly 4,000 miles from Moscow, they had reached the eastern limit of the Asian main-

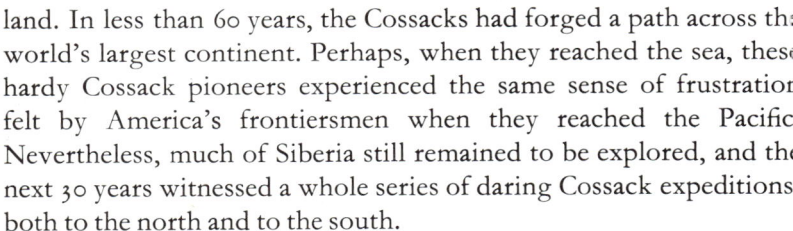

Above left: a drawing of a shaman of the Tungus tribe, one of the most numerous groups in Siberia, from a book published around 1810. The shamans were medicine men, who knew something about medicinal herbs, but did most of their healing by means of dancing, dressed in elaborate clothing made of leather strips, with bells and cymbals attached.
Above: a tribal Siberian sorceress.

land. In less than 60 years, the Cossacks had forged a path across the world's largest continent. Perhaps, when they reached the sea, these hardy Cossack pioneers experienced the same sense of frustration felt by America's frontiersmen when they reached the Pacific. Nevertheless, much of Siberia still remained to be explored, and the next 30 years witnessed a whole series of daring Cossack expeditions, both to the north and to the south.

In 1648, a small fleet commanded by a Cossack named Deshnef traveled north along the Kolyma River to the East Siberian Sea on the north coast of Asia. Following the coast, Deshnef reached and rounded the extreme northeast tip of the continent and, according to some sources, may even have explored the coast southward around the spoon-shaped peninsula now known as Kamchatka.

Meanwhile, other Cossacks were blazing a trail southeast through the uplands to an important river called the Amur, the northern-most limit of the great Manchu Empire of China. In 1644, the Cossack Poyarkov followed the river northeastward to its mouth on the Sea of Okhotsk. In 1650, he was followed by a band of Cossacks under a bold adventurer named Khabarov. This group not only reached the

Above: Cossack troops in Switzerland in the year 1799, depicted in a gouache dated 1802 by Wilhelm von Kobell. The Cossacks retained their vigorous enjoyment of life wherever they went. This painting shows them dancing to music played by a band of their enemies, the French, on the opposite bank.

Amur River, but also traveled down its length, attacking villages along the way in the name of the czar. Word of Khabarov's maneuvers soon reached the Manchus, and a force of Chinese soldiers was sent to oust the invaders. But on this—and on several subsequent occasions—the Cossacks succeeded in routing the Chinese. For the moment, the Russians were in possession of the mighty river. To assert their claim, they built settlements along its banks and sent embassies southward to negotiate at the court of the Manchu rulers in Peking.

The Manchus, however, remained adamantly uncooperative, and in 1685 launched a full-scale attack on the Russian settlements in the Amur River Valley. Despite heroic resistance, the Cossacks were defeated and forced to evacuate the area. Five years later, by the Treaty of Nerchinsk, Russia officially gave up its claims to the eastern Amur River Valley. But there was one compensation. The treaty included a proviso granting the Russians certain trading rights in China. Russian merchants were quick to take up this offer, and

soon, caravans loaded with Chinese silks, bales of tea, and carefully packed porcelain were winding their way westward, through the deserts, steppes, and mountains, to Russia.

And what of Russia itself during this century of Siberian exploration and expansion? The "Time of Troubles" had come and gone, but still the nation remained bogged down in ignorance and tyranny. Serfdom was even more widespread and oppressive, and the czars continued to rule with an iron hand. Only the Cossacks retained real freedom and scope for action—both within the country and outside its borders. Not for them the prohibitions against travel outside of Russia. They cheerfully accepted offers from foreign governments to serve as mercenary soldiers, and took part in many a great battle in Western Europe. In 1683, for example, they helped the Poles drive an invading Turkish army away from the besieged city of Vienna.

By far the most dashing and notorious Cossack in Russia at this time was a man named Stenka Razin. Exceptionally tall and strong, he practically became a legend in his own time for his daring exploits and his scorn of all authority. He led his men on brazen daylight raids up and down the Volga, and everywhere he went attracted flocks of loyal followers who called him *Batushka* (father).

Right: a group of Siberian merchants entertaining Chinese traders in the border town of Kyakhta. After the Treaty of Kyakhta of 1728, the border towns of Kyakhta and Nerchinsk became the two official stations for Russian trade with China.

His deeds both delighted and terrified the common people, for no one knew where he might strike next.

In 1670, Stenka arrived in Tsaritsyn (now Volgograd) and quickly won to his side a large number of officers and men from the czar's own army. When the czar sent another army against him, the deserters from the first infiltrated the second, and persuaded the soldiers to throw their officers into the river and join up with Stenka. The Cossack leader greeted his new troops with an impassioned speech of welcome: "At last my friends, you are free; what you have just done

Right: "The Siege of Vienna in 1683," by Franz Geffels. The Cossacks became famous for their skill as mercenary soldiers, and when the papal nuncio in Cracow reported that Cossacks in the Polish service were coming to relieve Vienna from the Turkish siege, he added they were "reckoned to be the best infantry which one can send against the Turks."

liberates you from the yoke of your tyrants. . . . It is to destroy them that Heaven has put you under my protection. Help me and we will finish what we have begun!''

Stenka Razin was not always so warlike. Sometimes he could be positively sentimental. On one of his southern raids, he had captured a Persian princess, whom he dearly loved. But one evening, while feasting in Astrakhan, he got very drunk and took it into his head that his affection for the girl would make the Volga jealous. After all, he told his companions, it was to the river that he owed his good

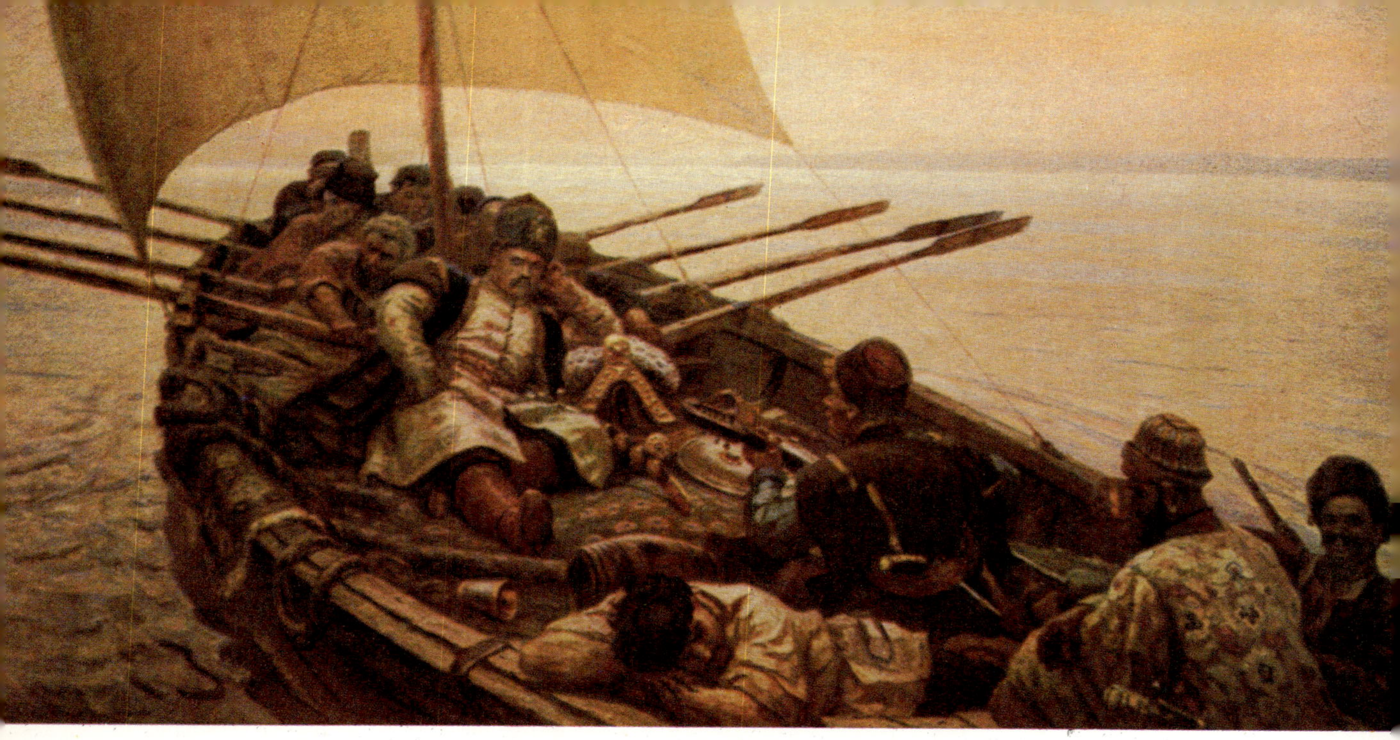

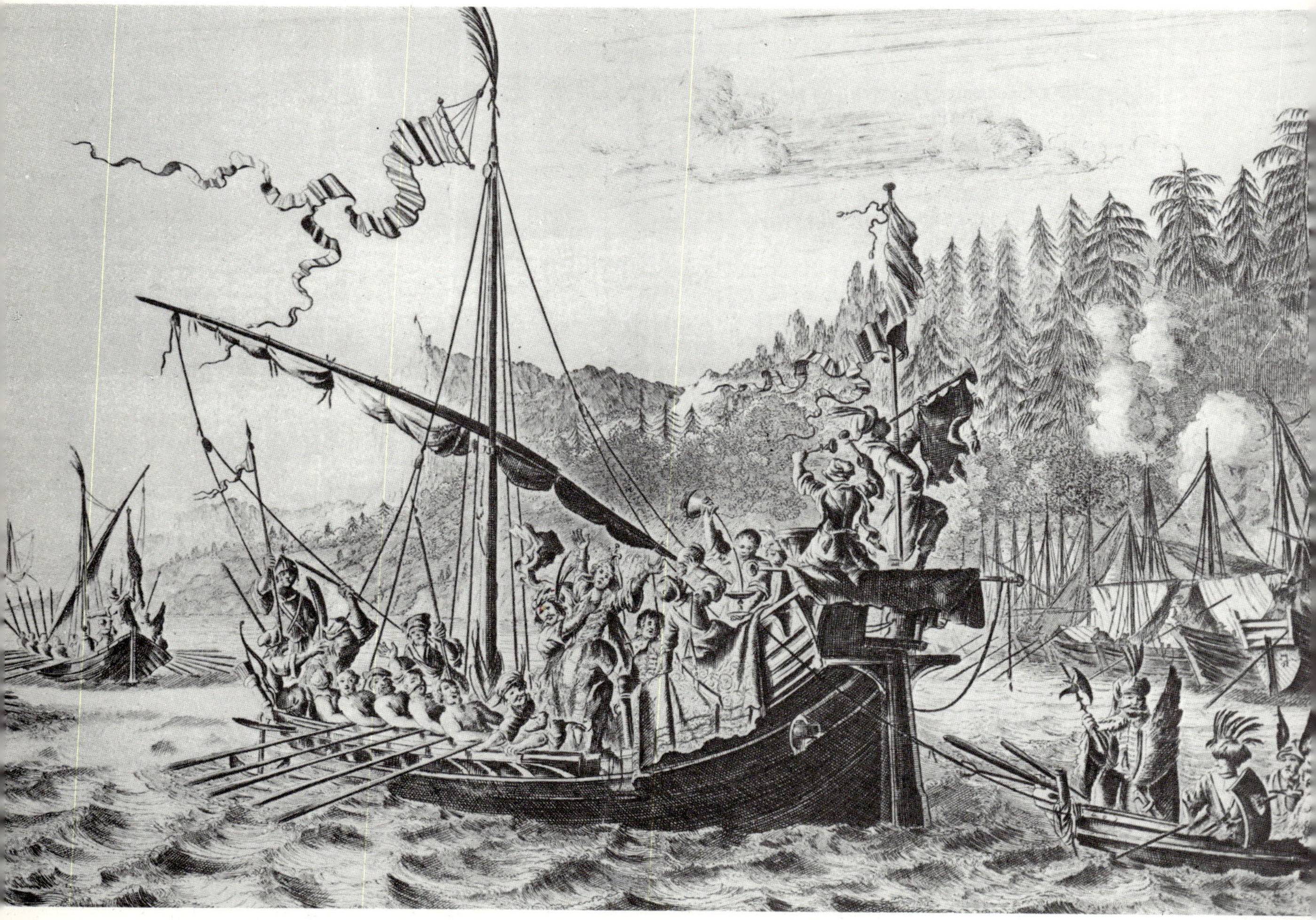

Left: the great Cossack Stenka Razin sitting in one of his longboats. A foreigner who met him described him as tall, well-built, a man who carried himself with dignity and haughtiness.

fortunes. Then, addressing the river, he said, "I seem to hear thy reproaches, that I have never given *thee* anything." Stenka paused for a moment. Then, with tears streaming down his face, he cried, "I offer thee with all my heart what is dearest to me in the world!" So saying, he seized the hapless princess and threw her into the river. There, weighted down with her jewels and golden robes, the poor girl sank to her death.

But such acts of reckless extravagance were not for the average Russian. Life for the common man was one of relentless, backbreaking toil, unrelieved by any hope of advancement. Russia had but two classes: the very rich and the very poor. It was not uncommon for estate owners to possess 100,000 serfs—men and women who slaved on the land year in and year out, and yet could not even call their miserable huts their own. Schools were unheard of, and even the rich were uneducated. Science and technology were still regarded with profound suspicion, and the whole Russian population remained as abysmally ignorant as it had been under Ivan the Terrible.

This was the state of affairs when Czar Peter I (later called Peter the Great) came to power in 1689. Peter, unlike his predecessors, was not content with things as they were. He wanted to modernize his benighted country and make it a great power along Western lines. As a boy, he had learned about the West from the foreign

Left: the drunken Stenka Razin throws his Persian princess from his ship into the waters of the Volga. This engraving of the incident is by the Dutch traveler Jan Struys, who was visiting the Cossack leader on his ship when the event occurred.

Right: Stenka Razin gathered a band of destitute Cossacks around him and they went out together on a rampage of reckless plundering that lasted for four years. Toward the end, Stenka began a "crusade" to rally the people against the boyars, whom he called traitors to the czar. His rebellion was finally crushed by the government and he and his brother, Frolka, shown here, were executed in 1671.

Left: a portrait of Peter the Great as a ship's carpenter's apprentice. During much of his journey throughout Europe he traveled incognito. This picture was painted while he was in The Netherlands.

merchants and ambassadors living in Moscow. His interest in the West never waned, and in 1697, he assembled a special delegation to travel through Europe and learn about Western technology and statecraft. This in itself was novel enough, but the most extraordinary aspect of the mission was that it included Peter himself. As Voltaire put it, "It was a thing unparalleled in history, ancient or modern, for a sovereign to withdraw from his kingdom for the sole purpose of learning the art of government."

The art of government, however, was not the only thing Peter was interested in. In The Netherlands, posing as a junior member of the Russian delegation, he hired himself out to a shipbuilder, and earned his living under the humble name of Peter Mikhailof. On receiving his

Right: an engraving made in 1748 of the speech Peter the Great made to William III of England in Utrecht in 1697. The speech reads: "Most Renowned Emperor. It was not the desire of seeing the celebrated Cities of the German Empire, or the most potent Republic of the Universe that made me leave my throne in a distant Country & my victorious Armies; but the vehement passion alone of seeing the most brave and most generous Hero of the Age. I have my wish & am sufficiently recompensed for my Travel, in being and admitted into your Presence; your kind Embraces have given me more satisfaction than the taking of Azoph & triumphing over the Tartars, but the conquest is yours; your Martial Genius directed my sword, and the generous emulation of your Exploits instill'd into my breast ye first thoughts I had of enlarging my dominions. I cannot express in words the veneration I have for your sacred person; my unparalleled journey is one proof of it . . . if either in peace or war your industrious Subjects will trade to the most northern parts of the world, the ports of Russia shall be free to them; I will grant them greater immunities than ever they yet had and have them enrolled among the most precious accorde of my empire, to be a perpetual memorial of the Esteem I have for the worthiest of Kings."

first salary, he remarked, "This will serve to buy me a pair of shoes, of which I stand in great need." Peter also studied shipbuilding in England before going on to Vienna to meet the German emperor. But there, news of trouble at home forced him to cut short his visit. He returned to Moscow, asserted his mastery over the nobles who had tried to seize power in his absence, and then set to work on his task of modernizing Russia.

He began his program by sending a large number of young Russians abroad to study. He encouraged them to take their wives with them, an idea that scandalized the conservative Russian Church. He next attempted to update the old-fashioned appearance of his people by issuing a *ukase* (royal order) that all coats be trimmed to

Left: a woodcut cartoon showing Peter cutting off the beard of one of his subjects. It was part of the relentless campaign to Westernize the Russians.

Right: Northern Asia. The map shows the journeys of England's first merchant-ambassadors to Russia, as well as the routes followed by the fearless Cossack adventurers and devoted scientists who explored Siberia.

Western length. Those who refused were forced to kneel on the ground while soldiers cut the cloth to the right length.

By another ukase, Peter demanded that the nobility and merchants shave off their beards. But beards were the hardest thing for the Russians to give up, and those who could afford it paid all manner of fines and "beard taxes" for the privilege of keeping them. The peasants and clergy were allowed to keep their beards for free. John Perry, an Englishman hired to build a canal for Peter, reported that his best carpenter shared with all Russians "a kind of religious respect and veneration for their beards." Forced to shave because Peter was coming to inspect the canal, the carpenter carefully saved his shorn beard so that ultimately he might be buried with it. In heaven, he said, he would show it to St. Peter as proof that he had been a good son of the Russian Orthodox Church.

Peter also created many schools and universities, and stipulated that landowners' sons could inherit their fathers' estates only if they could read and write Latin or a modern European language.

Peter's most cherished ambition was to procure for Russia what he called "a window on the West"—a strip of land along the Gulf of Finland. In the early 1700's, after a bitter war with Sweden, he gained what he wanted, the coastline of Livonia and southern Finland. There, at great cost—both in lives and in money—he built a splendid new capital, which he called St. Petersburg (now Leningrad).

Peter also took a keen interest in Russian holdings to the east,

Left: the centenary celebrations in
St. Petersburg, 100 years after Peter
had built the magnificent new city.
The Admiralty Bridge, a bridge of boats,
leads to Falconet's statue of Peter.

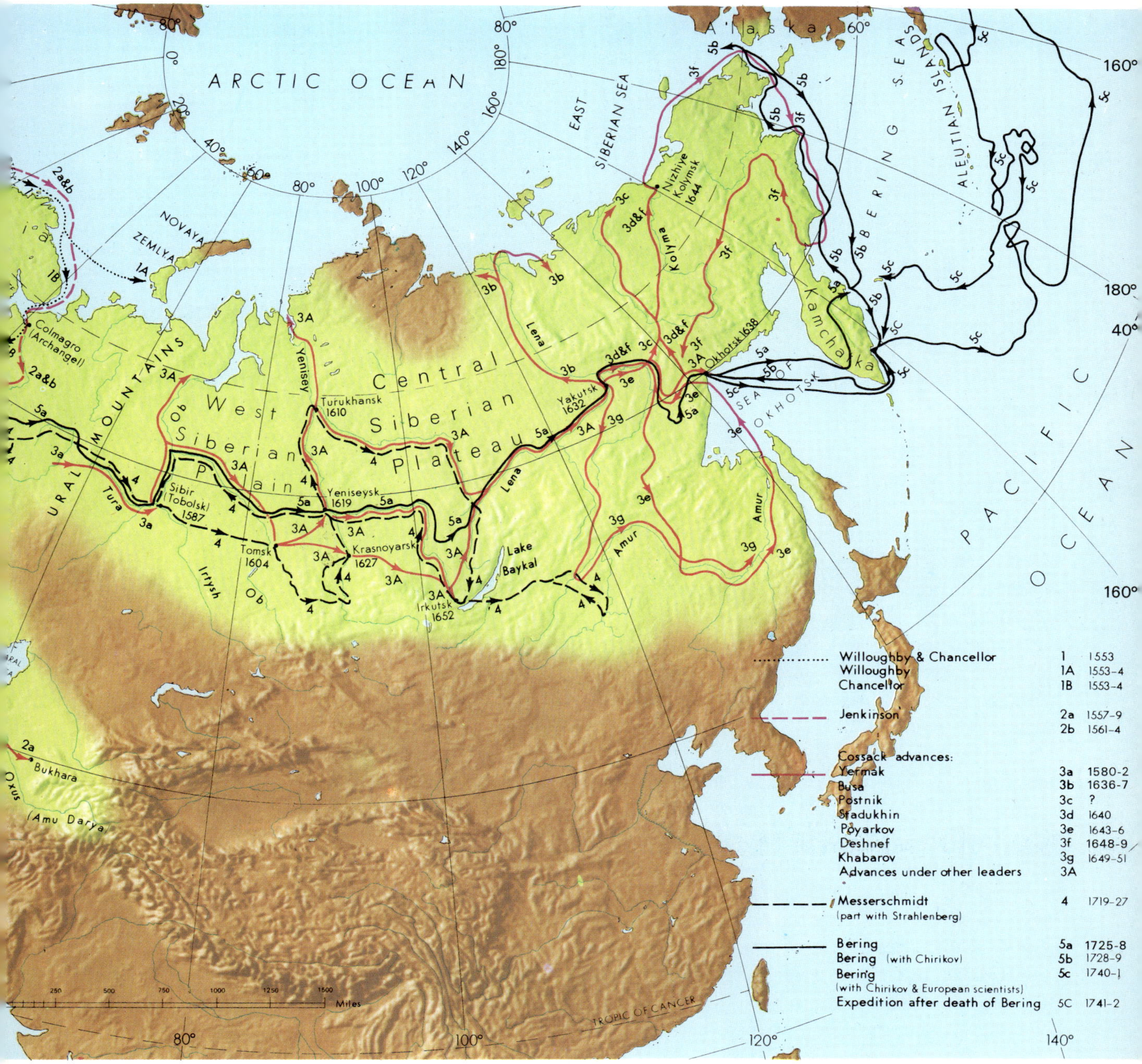

ARCTIC OCEAN

NOVAYA
ZEMLYA

Colmagro
(Archangel)

URAL MOUNTAINS

West
Siberian
Plain

Central
Siberian
Plateau

EAST
SIBERIAN SEA

A l a s k a

B E R I N G   S E A

ALEUTIAN ISLANDS

Nizhniye
Kolymsk
1644

Kolyma

Kamchaka

Okhotsk 1638

SEA OF OKHOTSK

PACIFIC
OCEAN

Yenisey

Turukhansk
1610

Lena

Yakutsk
1632

Lena

Amur

Sibir
(Tobolsk)
1587

Tura

Tura

Irtysh

Ob

Tomsk
1604

Yeniseysk
1619

Krasnoyarsk
1627

Lake
Baykal

Amur

Irkutsk
1652

Bukhara

Oxus
(Amu Darya)

Willoughby & Chancellor	1	1553
Willoughby	1A	1553-4
Chancellor	1B	1553-4
Jenkinson	2a	1557-9
	2b	1561-4
Cossack advances:		
Yermak	3a	1580-2
Busa	3b	1636-7
Postnik	3c	?
Stadukhin	3d	1640
Poyarkov	3e	1643-6
Deshnef	3f	1648-9
Khabarov	3g	1649-51
Advances under other leaders	3A	
Messerschmidt	4	1719-27
(part with Strahlenberg)		
Bering	5a	1725-8
Bering (with Chirikov)	5b	1728-9
Bering	5c	1740-1
(with Chirikov & European scientists)		
Expedition after death of Bering	5C	1741-2

250 500 750 1000 1250 1500
Miles

TROPIC OF CANCER

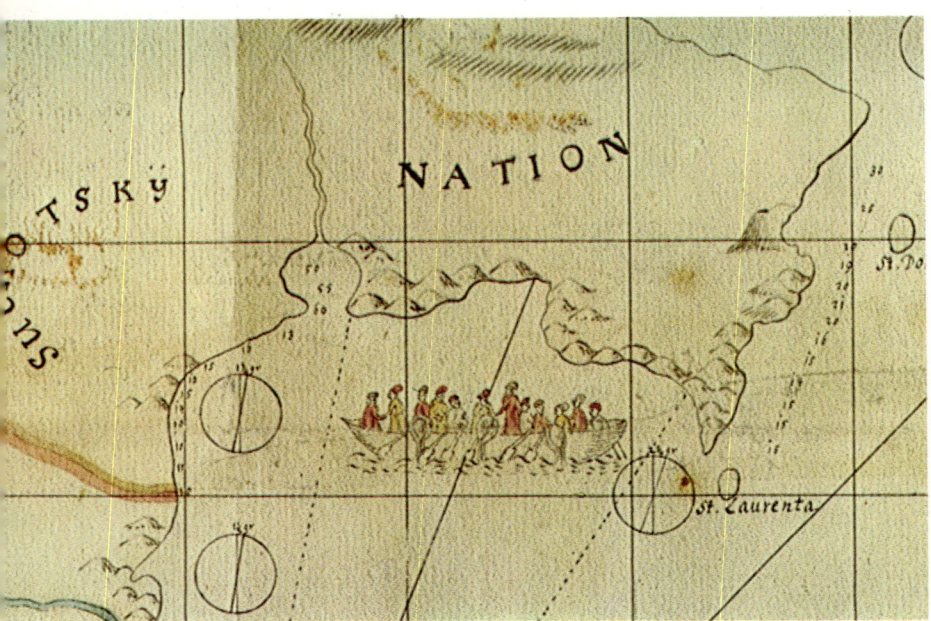

and it was he who prompted the first scientific exploration of Siberia. He wanted a comprehensive survey of his Asian dominion—its terrain and precise extent, its people and resources, its plants and animals. Peter did not hesitate to make use of foreigners to obtain the information he wanted. In the early 1720's, for example, he employed a Swedish adventurer named Strahlenberg and a Prussian naturalist named Messerschmidt to explore and map the Ob and Yenisey river valleys.

But Peter's greatest curiosity was about the mysterious Kamchatka Peninsula. Did this easternmost sector of Siberia join up with northwestern America, or was there a sea in between? In 1725, Peter, now ill and on the point of dying, summoned the Russian admiral Apraxin to discuss the matter. "I have been thinking over the finding of a passage to China through the Arctic," he said. "On the map before me there is indicated such a passage bearing the name Anian. There must be some reason for that. Now that the country is in no danger, we should strive to win for her glory along the lines of the Arts and Sciences." The "Anian" passage Peter was referring to was the Bering Strait, between northeast Siberia and western North America. It was Peter's wish that the Danish navigator

Vitus Bering sail northward up the coast of Kamchatka to see if such
a passage existed.

All the supplies for the voyage—stores and rigging, canvas and
ironwork—had to be hauled over the Siberian steppes and uplands,
and ships built along the eastern coast of Kamchatka before Bering
could begin his explorations. When at last he started out, he followed
the east coast of the peninsula northward until he reached the strait
that now bears his name. There, within sight of Alaska, severe gales
forced him to turn back. But he had accomplished his mission.
The nature of the territory between northeast Asia and northwest
America was now known.

Scientific exploration in Siberia did not stop with the death of
Peter the Great. In 1740, Bering headed another major expedition to
the farthest reaches of Siberia. Among its members were many distinguished European scientists: the French astronomer De la Croyère,
the German historian G. F. Muller, and the German naturalists
Johann Georg Gmelin and Georg Wilhelm Steller. The work of
these men, and of Bering himself, contributed vastly to the growing
body of knowledge about Siberia's geography, people, and resources.

Later in the 1700's, another series of important expeditions was launched by Catherine the Great. Imperious and tyrannical, this empress talked a lot about "enlightened rule," but did little to improve conditions in Russia. Indeed, the true extent of her "enlightenment" is shown by the fact that serfdom became almost universal in Russia during her reign. Nevertheless, she did recognize the value of science, and maintained the close association with the French Academy of Sciences that Peter had initiated early in the 1700's.

Peter's daughter, the Czarina Elizabeth, had made good use of this scientific body in 1760, when she requested the services of a French

Below: one of the midsummer camps of the abbé Chappe d'Auteroche, returning from Tobolsk to St. Petersburg after observing the transit of Venus.

Right: the famous Russian baths, much like the modern Finnish sauna. Nearly every traveler to Russia reported them, and even D'Auteroche said that they had a beneficial effect on the people, although he himself found, after one attempt at the bath, that the extreme heat of the steam was unbearable.

astronomer to observe the planet Venus as it passed close to earth the following spring. The astronomer, Chappe d'Auteroche, was to travel to Tobolsk in Siberia, where, on June 6, 1761, the planet's passage "could be viewed with more advantage than anywhere else."

Chappe d'Auteroche was a scholarly abbé, unused to travel, and he found the carriage journey through Russia extremely arduous. On one occasion, the snow was so deep that his carriage, breaking through the icy crust into a hole, "disappeared all at once, so that the horses' heads could but just be seen and we were buried!" The abbé and his companions, clutching their precious instruments, got out through a hole in the roof, and pulled the carriage out of the snow. With this experience behind them, the carriage was converted into a sledge, and they were swept along through gloomy forests and across glittering frozen rivers eastward to Siberia.

All this time, the abbé was worried that he might not reach Tobolsk in time. His most anxious moments came when he was only 200 miles from his destination. The spring thaws were beginning, and the countryside was "overwhelmed with torrents pouring down on all sides." Ahead lay a large river, which his drivers refused to cross because the ice was already cracking. But the abbé had come too far to be turned back by a mere river. He promised his men double pay if they would take the risk, and frantically plied them with brandy until they agreed. They crossed the river safely, and D'Auteroche reached Tobolsk in plenty of time to set up his telescope and observe the planet's passage.

This kind of dedication to science took many other frail scholars deep into the Siberian wilds in the decades that followed. But however brave, the scientists of the 1700's could never match the sheer, reckless courage of the men who had stormed across the continent 200 years earlier. The first, vital step in Siberia's exploration had been taken by the Cossacks—rebels, outlaws, and soldiers of fortune who neither knew nor cared about "scientific method."

Below: a detail from a Persian rug made in the 1500's that shows mysterious foreigners sailing in a ship. The Portuguese established a monopoly of trade with Persia by taking the port of Hormuz in 1514.

Persia, Gateway to the East

3

While the Cossacks were sweeping across Siberia, a hardy band of European merchants and adventurers were opening up another of Asia's hidden corners. This was the kingdom of Persia (now called Iran), tucked away between the Caspian Sea and the Persian Gulf in southwestern Asia.

A rugged land of mountains and narrow valleys, high plateaus and sweltering deserts, Persia was almost as forbidding as Siberia. Nonetheless, it had an irresistible appeal for Western travelers in the 1500's and 1600's. Located at the very crossroads of East and West, it offered exciting possibilities for trade. And, just as important, it possessed all the mystery and glamour of an utterly foreign world.

Before the 1500's, Europeans knew very little about Persia. For hundreds of years, the caravan routes connecting it to the Mediterranean had been jealously guarded by the Moslems, who possessed an exclusive monopoly over all trade with the East. Europeans did know that Persia was a vital link in the chain of sea and land routes by which the Moslems brought precious stones and spices from India and the Orient to Mediterranean markets. They also knew that Persia itself was the source of many luxuries: raw silk and dyes, wines and perfumes, delicate paintings, and rich brocades embroidered with roses, tulips, and lilies. Such luxuries suggested that Persia might be a fairy-tale land of Eastern romance. But was it? Fear of the Moslems—and of the unknown—had long kept all but a few Europeans from traveling east to find out.

And then, suddenly, early in the 1500's, the gates to Persia were flung open by the Portuguese. Using their new-found sea route around the tip of Africa, they sailed into the Persian Gulf and captured the strategic port of Hormuz in 1514. For the Portuguese, gaining control over this vital Persian port was just one step in their plan for acquiring a monopoly over all the Oriental spice trade. But for other Europeans, it signaled the start of a whole new interest in Persia. If the Portuguese could outflank the Moslems by approaching it from the south, why couldn't other traders accomplish the same end by approaching it from the north?

The English were the first to try. In 1561, flushed with their success in Russia, the governors of the Muscovy Company sent their first merchant to Persia. This pioneer trader was Antony Jenkinson —the same Antony Jenkinson who, in 1558, had traveled from Moscow to Bukhara in search of Cathay. This time, his mission was to investigate the rumour that "raw silk is as plentiful in Persia as flax is in Russia"—and, hopefully, to interest the Persians in trade.

With the blessing of the Russian czar, Jenkinson journeyed from Moscow to Astrakhan and boarded a ship bound for the southern shores of the Caspian Sea. On the way, a fierce seven-day storm nearly wrecked the vessel, and the captain was forced to make a landing halfway down the Caspian's west coast. Jenkinson—no doubt thankful to be safely back on dry land—unloaded his cargo of woolens, and hired a caravan to take him southward.

Below: Jenkinson's map, engraved in 1562, showing "Russia, Muscovy, and Tartarie." It shows his route down from Moscow to Astrakhan and across the Caspian Sea to Persia. The pictures are based on Marco Polo's accounts.

His first stop was the city of Shamakha, capital of a small Persian principality called Shirvan. The local ruler, Abdullah Khan, soon learned of his arrival, and asked to see him. When Jenkinson entered the palace, he found the khan seated in an elegant pavilion decorated with carpets of silver and gold. Surrounded by courtiers, the khan himself was the very picture of Eastern opulence. Jenkinson described him as being "richly apparelled with long garments of silk and cloth of gold, embroidered with pearls . . . his earrings had pendants of gold . . . with two rubies of great value set in the ends."

Below: an Indian miniature showing Abdullah Khan, who befriended Antony Jenkinson. When he saw Jenkinson sitting cross-legged before him, he ordered a stool so that Jenkinson could sit comfortably.

57

Above: a Persian miniature of 1590–1600 showing a man grooming one of the royal horses. Sometimes they were kept in solid gold stables, and equipped with jewel-studded gold saddles.

The khan took an immediate liking to the adventurous Englishman, and entertained him royally for several weeks. Jenkinson was treated to lavish banquets that sometimes consisted of as many as 290 different dishes, and learned to like coffee, a drink then unknown in Europe. Jenkinson was favorably impressed with everything about this glamorous way of life, except the harem system, which made it possible for princes such as the khan to have numerous wives. This not only shocked Jenkinson's sense of propriety, but also struck him as dangerous to the safety of the state. The more wives a man had, the more potential heirs he produced, and, as Jenkinson shrewdly observed, "one brother seeketh always to destroy another, having no natural love among them, by reason that they are begotten of divers women." In fact, this was a grave problem in the courts of Persia, and only one solution had been found: to keep male heirs cooped up in the women's quarters, thereby preventing them from learning anything about the arts of war.

From Shamakha, Jenkinson made his way 300 miles south to Qazvin, then the capital of Persia. All along the way, he encountered tribes of nomads. He described them as "pasturing people, which dwell in the summer season upon mountains, and in winter . . . re-

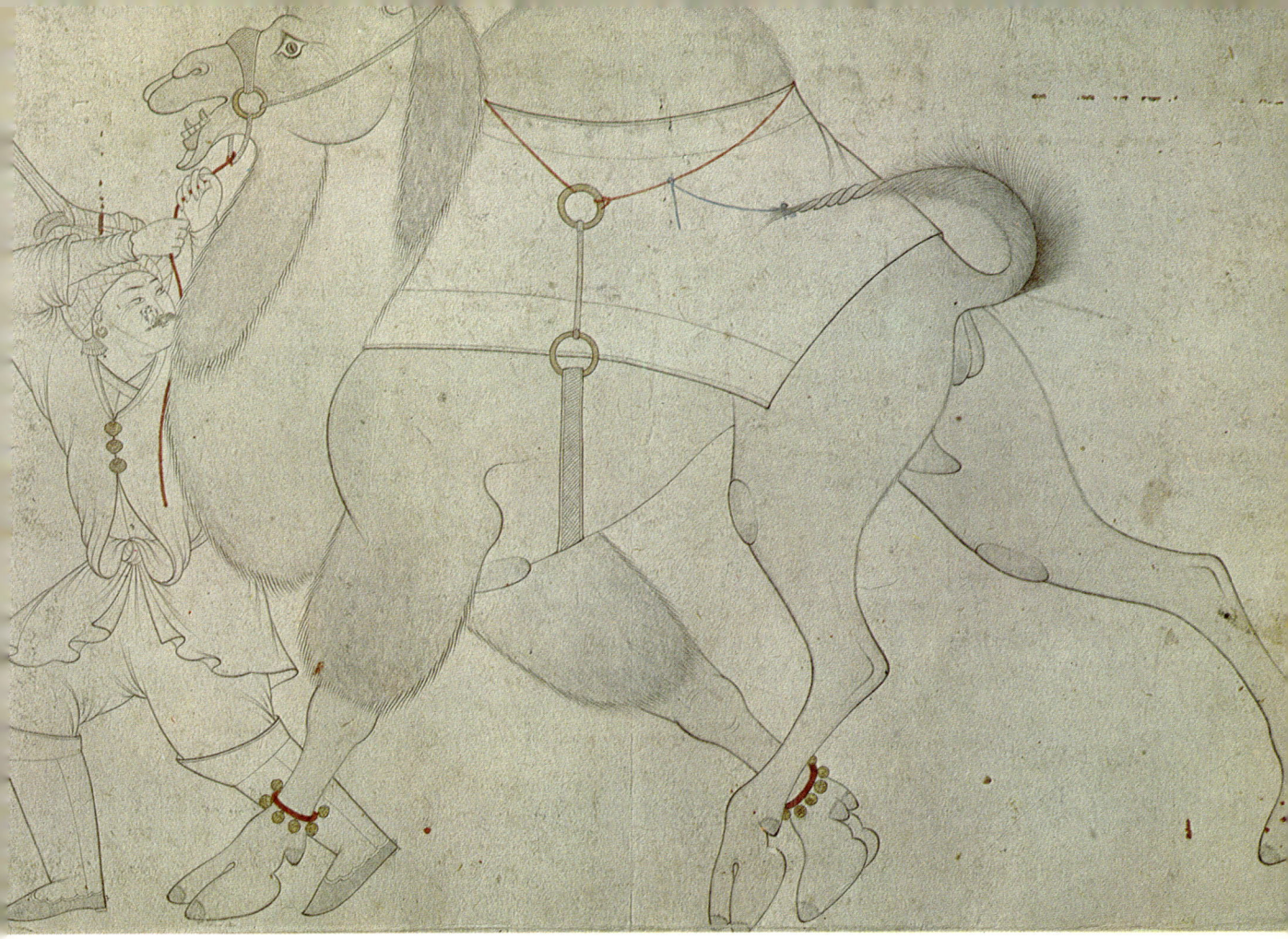

move into valleys, without resorting to towns or any other habitation." Possessing little but their flocks and their threadbare tents, these hardy tribesmen were a far cry from the luxury-loving courtiers Jenkinson had met at Shamakha.

The palace at Qazvin was, if anything, even more sumptuous than Abdullah Khan's. But the Persian king, Shah Tahmasp, was far less friendly than the khan. Jenkinson had barely presented his letter of introduction from Queen Elizabeth when the shah demanded to know his religion. When the merchant confessed that he was a Christian, the shah—who, like most Persians, was a Moslem—flew into a rage. "Oh thou unbeliever," he cried, "we have no need to have friendship with the unbelievers!" So saying, he ordered Jenkinson to leave his palace, instructing a retainer to follow him out and "purify" the ground he had walked on with fresh sand.

But Jenkinson was not one to give up easily. He stubbornly remained in Qazvin for several months, despite ugly rumors that the shah was thinking of sending his head as a present to the Sultan of Turkey. In the end, Jenkinson's friend Abdullah Khan intervened in his favor, and somehow even managed to convince the shah that it would do no harm to let the Englishman trade in his country.

Above: a Persian miniature, probably of the early 1500's, showing a camel with his driver. Horses were only for royalty—the ordinary people relied on the camel for all their traveling.

Jenkinson returned in triumph to Moscow late in 1562 with a rich cargo of silk and brocades, brilliant dyes and precious stones.

Over the next 20 years, the Muscovy Company sent five further missions to Persia over the route Jenkinson had pioneered. But none of them proved as successful as his had been, and the toll in lives was considerable. The northern route to Persia was fraught with perils for the unwary traveler: storms and pirates on the Caspian Sea, and the prevalence of plague in the region just south of it. By 1581, the English were beginning to consider a daring alternative route to the land of the shahs—via the Middle East.

The first English merchant to explore this possibility was John Newberry. Early in 1581, he crossed the deserts of present-day Syria and Iraq to the broad Tigris River. Following the river southward, he reached the Persian Gulf, and traveled down its eastern shores to the great port of Hormuz. There, under the very noses of the suspicious Portuguese, he spent six weeks gathering information about the "trade and custom of the place." He then traveled widely through the interior of the country and, on his return to England, gave a glowing report of the merchandise to be found in the bustling bazaars of Persia's cities.

But few merchants were willing to undergo the hardships of desert travel to reach these cities. After Newberry's travels, some years passed before Persia again became the object of a major English expedition. This time, the travelers were not merchants, but "gentlemen-adventurers"—24 European gentlemen under the leadership of two brothers named Sir Anthony and Sir Robert Sherley. They visited Baghdad, then crossed the Zagros Mountains into Persia and headed straight for Qazvin in hopes of meeting the shah.

They were not disappointed. Their arrival in the city coincided with the triumphant return of Persia's new young ruler, Shah Abbas I, from a successful campaign against a warlike tribe in the north. The shah's festive entry into Qazvin made an impressive sight. One of the Englishmen, John Manwaring, reports that at the head of the returning army rode 1,200 horsemen, "carrying 1,200 heads of men on their lances, and some having ears of men put on strings and hanged about their necks. . . . Then a good distance after them came the king, riding alone with a lance in his hand . . . being a man of low stature, but very strongly made, and swarthy of complexion. Next . . . came [the] lieutenant-general of the field, and all his bows

Right: rebellious tribesmen being burned, one of the sights witnessed by the Sherley expedition. They were amazed by the examples of casual savagery they often saw during their Persian tour in search of adventure.

Below right: a Persian picture of a captive Mongol. Not all the prisoners of war were mutilated or killed; many were kept as slaves. Here such a prisoner is shown in a symbolic form of restraint, that leaves his right hand free.

Above: Sir Robert Sherley, painted by Sir Anthony van Dyck while he and his wife were in Rome in 1622. Sherley posed in his turban and Persian cloak and tunic.

[archers] in rank like a half-moon to the number of 20,000 soldiers."

The Sherley brothers, as leaders of the English party, soon gained an audience with the shah. Telling him that they were English knights anxious to enter his service, they presented him with a tribute of gems and a golden goblet. Pleased and flattered, the shah gave them in return "40 horses all furnished, two with exceeding rich saddles plated with gold and set with rubies and turquoises."

The English party remained five months in Persia and were held in high esteem by the shah. The Sherleys soon rose to a position of prominence in the Persian court. In 1599, Shah Abbas sent Anthony

Above: Teresa, the Persian princess that Robert Sherley married, painted by Van Dyck. They had stopped in Rome on their way to England, hoping to interest European powers in Persia.

Sherley as his ambassador to Europe to arrange a European alliance with Persia against their common enemy, the Turks. Anthony's mission was a complete failure, and he did not return to Persia. Robert Sherley, who had remained with the shah as a sort of hostage, was left in a very awkward position. He began writing mournful letters to his brother telling him that he had given up all hope of "delivery out of this country."

But Robert's time in Persia was not a complete loss, either for himself or for the shah. The young Englishman met and married a lovely Persian princess named Teresa, and began advising the shah on military matters. With Sherley's help, the shah reorganized his army, using European strategy against the Turks with great success.

In gratitude, the shah made Sherley his new ambassador. Between 1609 and 1627, Robert and his wife traveled around the courts of Europe, vainly trying to interest various monarchs in a military alliance with the shah. But despite his lack of success, Robert Sherley loyally returned to Persia. Over the years, he had come to regard the kingdom as his real home, and Shah Abbas as his closest friend. But in 1628, the shah repaid his years of devotion and service with a cruel rebuff. He publicly rejected the Englishman "wishing Robert Sherley to depart his kingdom as old and troublesome." This unfeeling declaration broke Sherley's heart, and a month later, he died.

There was a definite streak of cruelty in the shah, and his treatment of Robert Sherley was nothing compared to the way he dealt with his own children. When word reached him that his eldest son had become popular among his people, the jealous shah had him put to death, and even ordered that the young man's head be brought to him as proof. Mercifully, Abbas's second son died of natural causes, but the third and fourth were not so lucky. They, too, incurred their father's wrath, and were both blinded.

But however barbaric he was as a father, Shah Abbas was remarkably progressive as a ruler. He had a genius for administration, and a keen eye for whatever would improve the efficiency of his government. One of his first acts as king was to build roads and bridges to link up the far-flung corners of his empire. The most famous of these causeways was the *Sang Farsh* (stone carpet), a road stretching almost all the way across northern Persia.

Abbas's most lasting monument, however, was the city of Isfahan. Located in the very heart of the kingdom on one of Persia's few

Right: Shah Abbas receives the envoy of Jahangir of India. Abbas was a great and skilled diplomat, and his court attracted many envoys from countries both to the east and west.

rivers, it became the shah's official capital late in the 1500's. At his command, Isfahan was almost completely rebuilt, and soon became one of the most beautiful cities in the East. The Persians were justly proud of their new capital. *Isfahan nusf-i Jihan*, they used to say: "Isfahan is half the world."

Leading into the center of the city were long avenues of trees bordered by gardens where little fountains sparkled in the sun. In the main square, or Maidan, were hundreds of market stalls over-flowing with exotic merchandise: spices from the Orient, diamonds from India, delicate metalwork from Arabia, and the very cream of

Persia's own products. The fruits and flowers sold in the Maidan made it a kind of garden in its own right, and the air was perfumed with the fragrance of peaches, apricots, limes, and quinces, roses, violets, hyacinth, and jasmine.

Overlooking the Maidan were two splendid buildings. On one side stood the Lutfallah Mosque, its huge dome encrusted with blue and green stones intermingled with gold. Opposite the mosque stood the royal palace, a sumptuous concoction of marble and alabaster, ebony and ivory. The rooms of the palace were decorated with paintings and fine enamels, and furnished with the softest of Persian carpets.

Above: the Great Mosque at Isfahan, the city that Shah Abbas made his capital. The large central court of the mosque surrounds a pool, and the covered areas have blue tiled floors to give the impression of cool water.

65

Isfahan was just one of the cities seen and admired by a young Englishman named Sir Thomas Herbert, who traveled to Persia in 1627. Five years before, the English had driven the Portuguese out of Hormuz and established their own foothold in the Persian Gulf. And so it was by ship that Herbert reached the country, landing at the port of Bandar Abbas, just north of Hormuz. Like the Sherleys, Herbert was a "gentleman-adventurer," and he set off eagerly to explore the kingdom. His journey, which took him all the way to the Caspian Sea and back again, gave him ample opportunity to observe Persian life and manners at close hand.

Herbert was particularly impressed by the gentleness and courtesy of the Persian nobility. They seemed to live a charmed existence, and showed surprisingly little interest in the world beyond Persia. If they asked Herbert any questions at all about Europe, it was only to know whether "such and such a country had good wine, fair women, serviceable horses, and well-tempered swords." Herbert surmised that it was their own good wine—and their indulgence in opium—that made them so complacent. "But above all," he wrote, "poetry lulls them, that genius seeming properly to delight itself amongst them."

But not all visitors to Persia were as favorably impressed with its people as young Herbert. John Chardin, a French merchant who visited the country in the late 1600's, wrote that "Luxury, sensuality, and licentiousness on the one hand, scholasticism and literature on the other, have made the Persians effeminate."

And another traveler, an English trader named John Fryer, who also visited Persia in the mid-1600's, found much to criticize. He complained bitterly about the climate which, he said, caused "rheumatisms, numbness, and periodical fevers," and scoffed at the Persian's naïve belief that washing in the public baths, or *hummums*, would cleanse them of their sins. Fryer was particularly critical of the reigning shah, Suleiman, who "ruled like another Nero." In fact, Suleiman—like many of the kings who succeeded Abbas—was extremely vicious. He delighted in torturing his wives, and thought nothing of putting out a man's eyes if he displeased him.

But even the wickedness of the shahs could not dim the rosy light in which most European visitors viewed Persia in the 1600's. By the end of the century, there were merchants from many different countries either living in the country or making regular journeys

66

Above: an engraving from a drawing by John Chardin, a diamond merchant, of the city of Isfahan. He spent many years living in Persia in the 1600's.

Left: an engraved portrait of Thomas Herbert. Herbert went on to India and Ceylon after his visit to Persia, returning to Europe in 1629.

through it on their way to India. Many wrote rhapsodic accounts of Persian life, and all agreed that it was the most civilized in the East.

Even so, European interest in Persia began to diminish late in the 1600's. Portuguese power in the Orient was rapidly waning, and the traders of England, France and The Netherlands increasingly focused their attention on India and the Far East.

This gradual shift in European interest was speeded up early in the 1700's, when a series of major upheavals made access to Persia all but impossible. In 1722, the kingdom was suddenly invaded by Afghan tribes from the east. It took the future shah, Nadir Kuli, eight years to drive them out. Under Nadir, Persia was rarely at peace, and late in his reign a series of rebellions, including that of the group of poor tribes called the Qajars, occurred.

The Muscovy Company chose this unhappy moment to send a merchant named Jonas Hanway to Persia. His task was to explore the possibilities of keeping open the old northern trade route to the kingdom. The expedition proved a disaster. Poor Hanway was

Above: John Fryer, a doctor who spent 9 years traveling through Persia and India. His *New Account of East India and Persia*, which was published in 1698, is one of the most interesting books describing the area at that time.

Right: Persian baths, as pictured in a Persian manuscript of 1566. It was these baths that Fryer was so skeptical about, reporting that the people firmly believed that washing there would be effective in cleansing them of sin.

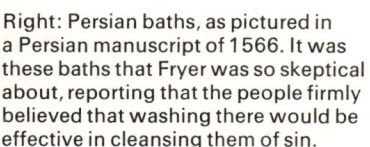

robbed by highwaymen, imprisoned by the Qajars, and almost coerced into running a harem by the shah. It was only with great difficulty that he finally managed to obtain compensation for the goods he had lost and make his way back to England.

"How happy Persia might be," Hanway wrote later, "if a general depravity of manners did not involve her inhabitants in such an inextricable confusion." Indeed, dynasties rose and fell in rapid succession in the war-torn country until the late 1700's. Then the Qajars themselves succeeded in producing a long-standing ruling dynasty. But by that time, the once-flourishing trade in Persian silk had dwindled away. European merchants, busy reaping a harvest of spice and treasure farther east, almost forgot about Persia. Even the English, who had done so much to pioneer new routes to the kingdom, paid it little heed in the second half of the 1700's. It was to take a whole new set of circumstances—the power-politics of the 1800's—to reawaken British interest in this exotic "gateway to the East."

Below: Jonas Hanway, painted by Arthur Devis. He unfortunately reached Astrabad just as it was captured by a rebel army, who took his merchandise and kept him locked in his lodgings. After his release he was nearly taken as a slave by highwaymen, and when he reached the shah in Hamadan, he was told he could only be compensated for his goods if he went back to Astrabad.

The Mysterious Land of Tibet

4

Left: the Potala, the Dalai Lama's residence, in the Tibetan capital of Lhasa. This painting, done in the 1200's, shows the original Potala. In the mid-1600's, the Fifth Dalai Lama had it razed to the ground, and built a new and grander edifice in its place. The new building was the one seen and admired by the missionaries and explorers of the 1700's and 1800's. But, though different in outward appearance, the later Potala served the same functions as its predecessor. It was not only a palace, but also a monastery and a well-defended fortress.

The search for new markets had led English merchants deep into Russia and Persia; the Mongol challenge had drawn the Cossacks into the wilds of Siberia. But the motive that launched the exploration of Tibet was neither trade nor conquest: it was religion. The first Westerners to venture into this forbidding mountain realm were Jesuit missionaries, members of a Catholic order called the Society of Jesus. Quiet, scholarly men, they were often frail in health and old in years. Yet their dedication led them to achieve feats of bravery and endurance worthy of the toughest Cossack.

The Jesuits began arriving in the Orient in the 1500's, soon after the Portuguese had pioneered the sea route to Asia. By 1601, the hardworking fathers had founded a flourishing mission at Goa, on the west coast of India, and another at Peking, in northern China. From these two centers, they ventured farther and farther afield, activated not only by missionary zeal, but also by a growing interest in exploration for its own sake.

In the early 1600's, the Jesuits working in northern India began to hear intriguing stories about a strange land called "Tibet" beyond the mountains. In this land, they were told, dwelt priests who

Right: a monastery in Tibet, hugging the hilltop over a vast expanse of a valley landscape. The Tibetans are a very religious people, and their monasteries—as in Europe during the Middle Ages—were the main centers of education and intellectual development.

dressed and behaved much like the Jesuits themselves. They wore long robes, never married, and performed rites that sounded strangely like baptism, confession, and communion. Rumors of a mysterious Christian community somewhere in Asia had haunted Europe for centuries. Could the people of Tibet be the famous lost Christians?

The Jesuits longed to follow up the lead, but the soaring Himalayan mountains between India and Tibet presented a daunting obstacle. And, as they learned from the few merchants who ventured north, the terrain on the other side of the Himalaya was no less formidable. In fact, the inner recesses of Tibet are all but inaccessible. Most of the country's 472,000 square miles are slung over the world's highest mountains, highest passes, and highest plateaus. Except for a few nomads, this barren, windswept region was uninhabited. Most of the population was concentrated in the southern part of Tibet, where there are pockets of lush green grazing and agricultural land in the troughs between the Himalaya. But even these lovely valleys are perched at heights greater than the mountain summits of most other countries.

Yet despite what they had heard—and guessed—about the perils of Himalayan travel, the Jesuits' desire to reach the tantalizing land beyond the mountains only increased as the years went by. The possibility that the Tibetans might not be Christians after all did not deter them. On the contrary, as one industrious father put it, "a great harvest of heathens may be reaped."

No Jesuit was more eager to reach Tibet than Father Antonio de Andrade, a 44-year-old priest working in northern India in 1624. One day, in the city of Delhi, he met a group of Hindu pilgrims bound for the holy shrine of Badrinath, deep in the Himalaya near the Tibetan border. Here at last was the opportunity he had been waiting for! Without a moment's hesitation, he and his companion, Brother Manuel Marques, collected two Christian Indian servants, donned Hindu garb, and joined the pilgrim caravan.

Slowly, the long column of men wound its way northward— through forests thick with leeches, leopards, and tigers; through fields luxuriant with wild flowers; through fragrant groves of lemon, cinnamon, and cypress trees—to the foothills of the Himalaya. The weather grew steadily colder, and the pilgrims' path, which now followed the Ganges River, became increasingly narrow and more

Above: a detail from a painting of the 1600's showing the Portuguese colony of Goa, on the coast of India. The vignette shows St. Francis Xavier arriving at the colony, which became the headquarters of missionary work.

Left: a contemporary portrait of Antonio de Andrade. He was convinced that hidden in the valleys of the Himalaya were pockets of forgotten Christians, and he was determined to make his way to the lost communities.

Right: a river gorge in the foothills of the western Himalaya. Father Antonio de Andrade traveled through this region on his journey to Tibet.

dangerous. Sometimes the travelers had to creep along ledges that were only inches wide, clinging to the rough side of the river gorge hundreds of feet above the swirling waters.

Some 150 miles north of Delhi, they came to the tiny Indian town of Srinagar. Something about Andrade and his servants aroused the suspicion of Srinagar's ruler, but he let them pass on to Badrinath. There, Andrade and his companions left the caravan and made for Mana, the last village in Indian territory. When they reached the village, they found that orders had been received from Srinagar to have them halted. But the Jesuit had come too far to be stopped now. Before him lay the Mana Pass, gateway to Tibet. When night fell, he and his servants escaped and headed for its summit.

Though it was summer, the pass was covered in snow so deep that the three men frequently sank up to their chests in it. At some points they could make their way forward only by lying prone on the snow and moving their arms and legs like swimmers. It was a terrifying ordeal, but they did not dare to stop, for to do so would have meant freezing to death. They lost all feeling in their hands and feet, and

Above: present-day lamas outside a lamasery in Ladakh. Bordering on Tibet, Ladakh had, before the Chinese occupation, very close educational and religious links with the lamaseries of Tibet, sharing their culture.

Right: Leh, the capital of Ladakh district in Kashmir where the 400 Christian converts were sent after their church in Tsaparang had been destroyed by the local lamas. The castle of the Leh kings is shown on the left. Azevado traveled there to beg for mercy for the Christian slaves.

Andrade in particular was so frostbitten that he knocked a finger off without feeling a thing. "Having no sense of pain I should not have believed it, had not a copious flow of blood shown it to be a fact!"

With the dawn came the glare of the sun on the snow, blinding the men so much that they could hardly see the ground in front of them. But somehow they managed to reach the summit of the pass and descend into the valley below. They found themselves in the town of Tsaparang, capital of the small Tibetan state of Guge. Andrade was conducted to the king, who received him kindly and took great pains to answer his religious questions. No, the Tibetans were not Christians; they were Buddhists. But, as the Jesuit learned, there *were* many fascinating similarities between the two religions. The Buddhist *lamas* (monks) not only performed baptisms and heard confession, but also observed fasts, officiated at weddings, and held Masslike ceremonies where they blessed sacramental bread and wine.

The king of Guge was a Buddhist too, of course, but he was so impressed by Father Andrade that he held Christianity in high esteem. Moreover, he asked the Jesuit to teach the faith to his people. Overjoyed, Andrade returned to India to arrange for a mission, and came back the next year with two other Jesuits. A church for the

Right: a lamasery of Likir in Ladakh. Endowed with a splendid view of the valley spread below it and the white-cloaked mountains in the distance, it looks as it did in the time of Azevado.

Below: vast caravans followed the old trading routes such as the one that Grueber and D'Orville traveled along. This Chinese roll painting of the 1600's shows part of one of these caravans.

"lamas of the West" was built near the king's palace, the foundation stone being laid on Easter Sunday, 1626.

During the next few years, the mission made 400 converts. In fact, all seemed to be going well in Tsaparang when Father Andrade left the city in 1629 to become the Jesuit superior at Goa. But shortly after his departure, disaster struck. The local lamas, furious at the Jesuits' growing power, rose up against the zealous king and overthrew him. Guge was taken over by the ruler of the nearby Kashmiri state of Ladakh, and the 400 converts were enslaved and sent to Leh, Ladakh's capital. The church was demolished, but its four missionaries were allowed to remain in Tsaparang.

When news of this catastrophe reached Andrade, he at once dispatched another priest to Tibet. The missionary, Father Francisco de Azevado, was to travel to Ladakh, visit the king at Leh, and persuade him to free his Christian slaves and permit the reopening

Above: a wood model of the chief lama of Bhutan, who was of the Red Hat sect, which was the traditional party. When Cabral and Cacella were in Shigatse, the Red Hats were locked in political combat with the Yellow Hats, the reform party. The Jesuits, aware of the air of tension, decided to seek counsel from their brethren.

of the Tsaparang mission. It was a daunting task, but the 53-year-old Azevado was a brave and determined man. He made his way to Tsaparang and from there followed a rough track through the mountains to Ladakh, 200 miles to the northwest. Along the way, he frequently had to cross yawning chasms by means of flimsy rope bridges. Just how terrifying this could be was described by another Jesuit, Ippolito Desideri, who journeyed to Ladakh some 84 years later: "From one mountain to the other two thick ropes of willow are stretched, nearly four feet part, to which are attached hanging loops of smaller ropes of willow about one foot and a half distant from one another. One must stretch out one's arms and hold fast to the thicker ropes while putting one foot after the other into the hanging loops to reach the opposite side. With every step the bridge sways from right to left, and from left to right. Besides this, one is so high above the river and the bridge is so open on all sides that the rush of water beneath dazzles the eyes and makes one dizzy."

Azevado had no experienced companions to help him on his way. When he came to such a bridge, he simply commended himself to God, took hold of the ropes, and kept praying till he reached the other side. He reached the capital, Leh, safely in October, 1631. Around the town he noted fields of barley and of wheat, roaming herds of sheep and muskdeer, and occasional apricot trees. In the capital itself lived some 800 families. They dwelt in terraced houses that seemed to melt into the slope of the little mountain on which the palace stood.

Twice Father Azevado went to see the king of Ladakh. He was a man of "stern appearance," but turned out to be sympathetic to the Jesuit's requests. The king promised to release his Christian slaves and agreed to allow the missionaries to remain in Tsaparang. The Jesuit, anxious to carry the good news to Father Andrade, remained in Leh only two weeks before returning to India.

However, the good news turned out to be false news. After Father Azevado's departure, the king broke his word and had the remaining Jesuits placed under house arrest. In 1635, the mission had to be abandoned altogether.

Meanwhile, 600 miles to the east, another mission had been established in the Tibetan city of Shigatse. By 1628, two brave Jesuits, Father Cabral and Father Cacella, had reached the area via the tiny Himalayan kingdom of Bhutan. But this route proved so treacherous that the Jesuits realized that, if the mission was to be successful, they would have to find better lines of communication with existing missions in India and Tibet. Soon, Father Cabral set off and found a longer but much safer route to a mission in northeast India. On this journey, he pioneered a new route over the mountains. The route—over some of the highest Himalayan passes— took him through Nepal, and he was the first European to visit Katmandu, the Nepalese capital.

At the same time, Father Cacella made a heroic, but unsuccessful attempt to reach the Tsaparang mission. Forced back by heavy snow, he turned southward, rejoining Cabral in northern India.

After they had reported to the Jesuit authorities, Father Cacella returned to Shigatse. Soon afterward, worn out by his travels, he died. After the death of his colleague, Father Cabral also returned to Shigatse, but was recalled to India in 1632.

Not until 1661 did the Jesuits again penetrate into the hidden recesses of Tibet. In that year, two intrepid Jesuit travelers not only entered Tibet, but did so from an entirely new direction: China. By the late 1650's, Dutch merchants had broken the Portuguese monopoly on trade with Asia, and armed Dutch vessels had begun blockading the ports of call along the coast of China. This made it impossible for the Jesuits at Peking to maintain contact with their headquarters in Rome. They saw only one solution: to find an overland route to the West.

The Peking authorities chose two young Jesuits for this dangerous task, John Grueber and Albert d'Orville. Grueber, an Austrian, and D'Orville, a Belgian, were both trained geographers. Laden with surveying equipment, the two set out from Peking in April, 1661, and followed an ancient caravan route that took them west to the Great Wall of China. This had been completed by the Chinese in the 200's B.C., in an effort to keep out marauding barbarians from Central Asia. Stretching from China's east coast to the Gobi Desert, it was some 1,500 miles long and, as Grueber noted, was wide enough at some points for six horsemen to ride abreast on it.

The Great Wall has excited the admiration of travelers for hundreds of years. Some years after Grueber and D'Orville saw it, for example, another Jesuit named Father Verbiest had occasion to travel many miles along its length and wrote enthusiastically to a

Above: the Great Wall of China, which Grueber and D'Orville had to pass on their long journey from Peking to find an overland route to the West. Here, the wall is about 21 feet thick at the bottom and the parapet is 18 feet high. There are watchtowers at intervals of several hundred yards. The wall was first linked together by the expanding Ch'in dynasty to keep out nomadic tribesmen from Central Asia.

Left: an engraving of the Potala of Lhasa, made in 1667 from sketches that Grueber made when he was in the city.

Right: an engraving of the Chinese emperor made by A. Kircher from a sketch by Grueber. Before Grueber left, Kircher, a Jesuit scholar, came to an arrangement that Grueber would keep a record of the journey which he would give to Kircher, who was then planning his monumental work, *China Illustrata*. Kircher's book, dated 1667, gave Grueber's story to the world.

Imperij Sino-Tartarici Supremus MONARCHA.

friend that, "The seven wonders of the world condensed into one could not be compared with it . . . . It is carried in many places over the highest summits of the mountains from East to West, and follows all the acclivities, towers of a lasting construction rising into the air at intervals of two bow-shots apart."

Grueber and D'Orville headed southwest after leaving the Great Wall. They entered Tibet, and toiled on for three months over its endless mountains and high plateaus. Only the occasional sight of a nomad's black felt tent gave any indication that there were other human beings in this bleak and terrible domain.

In October, 1661, the two Jesuits reached Lhasa. This city had been the real heart and capital of Tibet for 20 years. In 1642, the Fifth Dalai Lama, head of the Yellow Hat sect, had invited a Mongol khan from the north to invade Tibet and, with his help, had subjugated the rival Red Hats. For the next 13 years, the khan and the "Great Lama" had ruled Tibet together, with the Mongol in charge of secular matters and the Dalai Lama in charge of religious affairs. But in 1655, the khan had died, and the lama had moved swiftly to assert his mastery over the political scene as well. A Mongol representative still lived in Lhasa, but he was completely subordinate to

Above: a prayer wheel. The use of these ingenious devices greatly interested Grueber. It is believed that when the small cylinder is spun the prayers on it are transmitted and it is not necessary to give any further thought or articulation.
Below: a man standing near two small buildings called *chortens,* little shrines dedicated to famous lamas, at which people may stop and pray.

the Great Lama, and played only a minor role in Tibetan politics.

At the root of the priest-king's power was the Tibetans' belief that the Dalai Lama was the reincarnation (reappearance on earth) of the great saint, Avalokitesvara, venerated by all the Tibetans. The Dalai Lama was held to possess special powers, and before his death was supposed to indicate the time and place of his next incarnation by mystical signs. Following these clues, a council of high priests would find a young boy, question him closely about his "previous life," and, when satisfied that he was indeed the reincarnation of the Dalai Lama, prostrate themselves before him. Thereafter, no one would dare question his exalted position as the semi-divine ruler of Tibet.

On entering Lhasa, Grueber and D'Orville were immediately struck, as all later travelers have been, by the sight of a majestic palace called the Potala, which overlooks the city. Begun by the Fifth Dalai Lama in 1642, this awesome structure is built into the side of a mountain, and its soaring walls appear absolutely impregnable. At the time of the Jesuits' visit, it served as a combination palace and monastery, for in addition to the Great Lama and his court, it housed hundreds of studious Buddhist monks.

Grueber was greatly impressed by the elegance of the courtiers he saw going to and from the Potala. But he was appalled by the appearance of the common folk in Lhasa's crowded streets. He found them astonishingly dirty and wrote later that "neither men nor women wear shirts or lie in beds, but sleep on the ground." Worse still, they "eat their meat raw and never wash their hands or face."

Grueber, like Andrade before him, was struck by the similarities between Christianity and Buddhism. But there were no Christian parallels for most of the religious practices he witnessed. One of these was the use of prayer wheels. These ingenious devices were designed to ensure the endless—and effortless—repetition of a prayer. They were cylindrical in shape, and could be turned by the wind, by a watermill, or by hand. Inside each cylinder was a scroll of parchment bearing the Sanskrit words *Om mani padme hum.* Literally translated, the phrase means "Oh, the jewel in the lotus," but for Buddhists it has a mystical meaning, and they believe that its repetition is pleasing to God.

Another custom Grueber saw in Lhasa was an annual rite in which the high priests selected a youth and gave him free rein for a day to slay whomever he wished. The young man, wearing "a very gay habit, decked with little banners, and armed with a sword, quiver, and arrows, wandered at will through the streets killing people at his pleasure—none making any resistance." Grueber's horror at this barbaric practice was not lessened when the Tibetans assured him that everyone slain in this way was guaranteed "eternal happiness."

The two Jesuits could stay only a short while in Lhasa; they had to get on before the winter snows closed the Himalayan passes. To

reach Nepal, they had to travel a torturous route through the Bhotia River gorge. At some points the trail became nothing more than a series of jutting stone slabs supported by iron pegs—1,500 feet above the foaming river! It took the Jesuits 11 days to navigate the 775 steps that made up this part of the trail.

In November, they reached Katmandu, and were immediately conducted to the Nepalese king. He was on the outskirts of the city with his army, preparing to repel an attack by a rebel tribe. Grueber made him a present of one of his telescopes. Looking through it, the king saw the distant enemy forces magnified many times and, thinking that they were upon him, ordered his astonished troops to attack at once!

The Jesuits finally reached Agra in March, 1662, 11 months after leaving Peking. There, worn out by his travels, D'Orville died. Grueber, however, pressed on—through what are now India, Pakistan, Iran, and Turkey—and eventually reached Rome, where he made his report to the pope.

Grueber and D'Orville were the last Jesuits to see Tibet in the

Above: a group of Tibetan musicians, elegantly dressed in the fashion that impressed Grueber. But he was appalled by some of their customs: the drums, for instance, made of human skin, and the famous Tibetan horns that were often made out of human leg bones.

still young men when they began their travels, and some – De Goes, Cacella, and D'Orville – died in the course of their work. Yet despite their relative frailty, each achieved remarkable feats of bravery and endurance, pioneering routes through forbidding terrain that even today remains a challenge for well-equipped explorers.

De Goes	1	1602–5
Messenger from De Goes to Ricci	1A	1605–7
Andrade	2	1624, 1625
Cabral & Cacella	3	1626–8
Cabral	3A	1628
Cacella	3B	1628
Azevado	4	1631–2
Grueber & D'Orville	5	1661–2
Desideri	6A	1713–4
Desideri & Freyre	6	1714–6
Freyre	6B	1716
Desideri	6C	1721–2
Desideri	6D	1725
Huc (with Gabet)	7a	1844–6
Huc	7b	1848–9

© Geographical Projects

1600's. But the authorities at Goa never quite gave up their dream of founding a permanent Jesuit mission in Tibet. In 1714, they took steps to realize that dream by sending two missionaries north to Leh, the capital of the Kashmiri district of Ladakh. The two men they chose made an odd pair. The nominal leader of the team was Emanuel Freyre, an experienced missionary in his mid-30's. His companion, Ippolito Desideri, was a young, enthusiastic priest not yet 31. It was Desideri who was to provide the real driving force behind the expedition.

The pair set out from Delhi in the autumn of 1714, intending to reach western Tibet by way of Kashmir. As they wound their way north through the Himalayan mountains, they often met shepherds tending flocks of sheep. These flocks provided the wool for the famous shawls made in Kashmir. Desideri described these lovely garments as being "so fine, delicate, and soft that, though very wide and long, they can be folded into so small a space as almost to be hidden in a closed hand."

The route through Kashmir to Leh involved terrible hardships. They were blinded by the glare of the sun on the snow, and often frightened out of their wits by the thunder of nearby avalanches. But they managed to reach their goal by June, 1715. Once there, Desideri

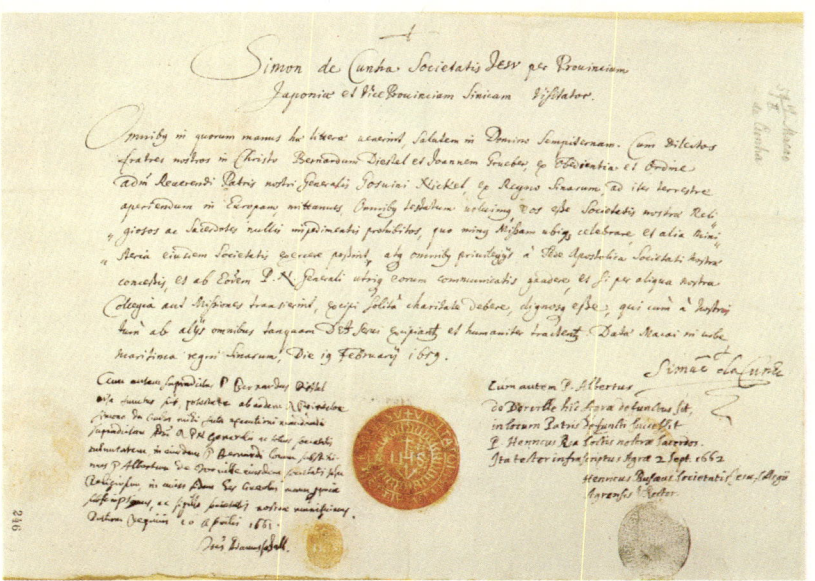

Left: a letter of patent given by Simon da Cunha, resident in Japan, to Grueber and Bernard Diestel (who was the man who had invited Grueber to join the China mission), charging them with finding a land route from Peking to Europe. This was the sort of license or passport that the Jesuits gave to their missionaries. In the lefthand corner, D'Orville's name was substituted for Diestel's, as Diestel had then died. In the righthand corner, Henri Roth's name is substituted for D'Orville's after his death in Agra in April, 1662.

was eager to begin the work of starting up a mission. But Father Freyre decided that he had had enough of Tibet already, and insisted that they return to India at once. Because Freyre was unwilling to go back the way they had come, the two set out to find an alternative route via eastern Tibet.

After several weeks of arduous travel, the pair managed to reach Gartok, a city some 75 miles southeast of Leh, and there they had a wonderful stroke of luck. A sizable caravan bound for Lhasa was just about to leave Gartok, and the Jesuits were invited to join it. Better still, the captain of this caravan was no rough barbarian, but a charming Mongol princess. She seems to have captured the heart of Freyre from the first moment when, "the Lady, whose pretty face was radiant with our gifts, raised her eyes to ours." Again and

Above: a caravan of traders in Ladakh making their way through the mountains. The difficult terrain such caravans had to negotiate can be seen here. Even in summer the mountains are covered with snow, and huge glaciers continually grind down into the valleys.

Left: an Indian miniature of Mount Kailas, showing the holy family of Siva and Parvati with their children Karthikeya and Ganesa, sitting in a cave. The mountain is holy to both the Hindu and the Buddhist faiths.

again in the course of the journey, she offered help and encouragement to the two travelers. Freyre recorded that "the terrible cold and wind would chafe my face so severely as to make me exclaim (I confess it) 'A curse on this cold!' But at such trying moments Princess Casals would comfort us with hot *cha* [tea] and . . . tell us to have courage, for no dangers from mountains or avalanches had power to harm us if we kept to her side."

Late in 1715, the party came in sight of Mount Kailas. This snowy Himalayan peak is the Central Asian equivalent to the Greeks' Mount Olympus, and is believed to be the abode of the gods. Hindu and Buddhist pilgrims from all over India and Tibet go to worship at this shrine and make a ritual trip around the base of the mountain, sometimes on their knees.

In March, 1716, the caravan reached Lhasa. Father Freyre set off at once for India, But Desideri, asserting his independence, decided to stay on in the Tibetan capital. Soon after his arrival, he gained admission to the imposing Potala palace. In the throne room he found himself confronting—not the Dalai Lama, as he had expected—but a Mongol king named Latsang. Following the death of the Fifth Dalai Lama in the late 1690's, the Mongols had descended on Lhasa and ousted the Great Lama's successor. Latsang, who had led the invasion, had installed himself as king and, with the help of

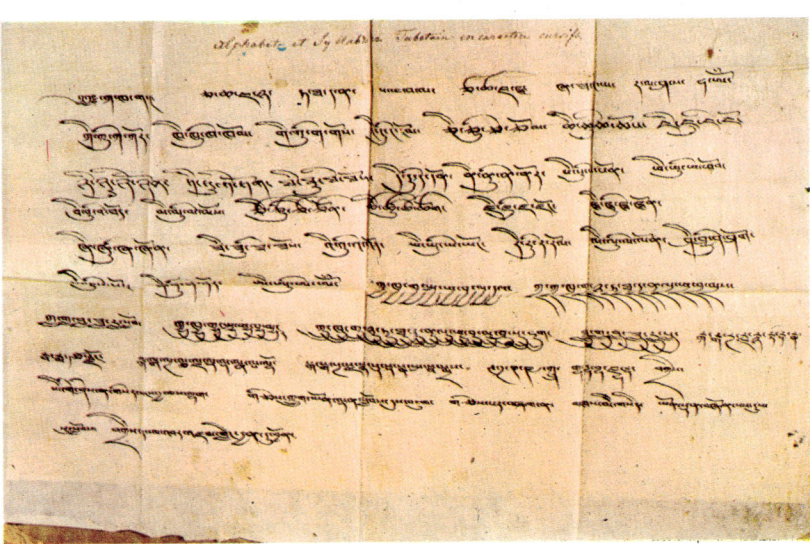

Right: the alphabet and syllables in Tibetan characters, a page from the material that Desideri brought back with him. He was the first European who learned to read and write Tibetan.

the Emperor of China, had won complete control over Tibet.

Desideri liked Latsang. He found him "by nature gay, joyous, and affable . . . courteous to all [and] easy to approach." The Mongol king was equally impressed by the young priest, and promised to look after him "as a father cares for his son." The king gave him permission to found a church in the city, but encouraged him first to study Buddhism, "the better to refute it."

Desideri retired to a lamasery (Buddhist monastery) outside of Lhasa and began studying the language and religious customs of Tibet. He was shocked by many of the things he learned. The Tibetans did not bury their dead, for example. Because they believed in the passage of souls from one creature to another, they fed their dead to eagles, dogs, even fish. They regarded this practice as an

affirmation of man's oneness with the universe, a means of uniting the dead person's soul with that of other, living creatures.

Another practice Desideri found astonishing was the belief that a man's innocence or guilt could be proved by a physical test. Alleged criminals were forced to plunge their hands into a cauldron of boiling oil in which there were two stones, one black and one white. If a man was innocent, he would be able to pluck out the white one without burning his arm. Needless to say, most of the accused were found guilty.

But the practices Desideri found most deplorable were the Tibetans' marriage customs. On the wedding day, the groom's friends fetched the bride—who, until that moment, did not know that she was to be married—and carried her kicking and screaming

Right: lamas wearing aprons made of human bones. The Tibetans' traditional attitude toward the bodies of their dead was one aspect of Tibetan culture that Desideri found hard to accept.

Above: a cup made from a human skull, which was used by the lamas for ceremonial religious occasions. Many of the customs that so amazed Desideri continued long after his time in Tibet.

to her future husband. In the presence of a lama, the groom smeared pats of butter on his bride's hair, officially making her his wife. But she was not only *his* wife—the ceremony automatically made her the wife of all her husband's younger brothers as well!

Desideri, appalled by these customs, addressed himself to the task of refuting them in a long tract that he wrote in Tibetan. But before he could get very far with his great work, a terrible calamity befell the capital. The Yellow Hat lamas had long resented King Latsang's usurpation of the Dalai Lama's power. In 1717, they connived with the ruler of a rival Mongol horde, the Dzungar Mongols, to drive him out. The Dzungars undertook the task with relish, and swept down on Lhasa to kill Latsang and sack the city. But, in turn, the Dzungars, too, were driven out by a large Chinese army in 1720. The Chinese came in the guise of religious crusaders, alleging that their mission was to reinstate the next Dalai Lama in his rightful place as ruler. In fact, what they did was to establish themselves as Tibet's "patrons," and installed Chinese representatives in Lhasa to "advise" the new young Dalai Lama.

During all this upheaval, Desideri had remained safely closeted away outside the city. When he emerged with his written refutation of Buddhism in 1721, all was calm again in Lhasa. But his book created quite a stir. "My house suddenly became the scene of incessant comings and goings," he wrote. Learned lamas from all over came "to apply for permission to see and read the book."

But Desideri's day of triumph in Lhasa was short. In early 1721, he received word that he was to leave Tibet. The pope at Rome had decided to give the missionaries of the Capuchin order (a branch of the Franciscans) the rights to carry on missionary work in Lhasa. Desideri, as a Jesuit, was forced to leave. Bitterly disappointed, the 36-year-old priest bade farewell to his friends in the capital and returned to India. He died, 12 years later, in Rome.

The success of the Capuchin mission in Lhasa signaled the end of the Jesuits' Tibetan ventures. Though the Capuchins, too, were soon forced out of the capital by more political upheavals, the Jesuits did not make any further attempts to found a mission there. In their own eyes, their missionary efforts in the mountain kingdom had been a failure. But in the eyes of the world, the courageous Jesuit fathers had achieved something just as important: they had laid the groundwork for all future exploration of Tibet.

Below: a Tibetan *thanka*, a painting
of a sacred subject that is hung in
a temple, showing a celestial being.
Thankas are normally done on cotton,
and are therefore known as cotton-
drawings. The drawing itself is then
lavishly framed in silks or brocades.

Central Asia: Desert Challenge 5

Sandwiched in between Tibet and Siberia lies the giant desert waste of Central Asia. Roughly triangular in shape, it begins just east of Kashmir, with the Taklamakan Desert, and gradually widens out into a vast complex of wastelands that includes the Dzungaria, the Ordos, and the mighty Gobi deserts of northern China and Mongolia. With the exception of its eastern fringes, the whole bleak region is enclosed and broken up by mountain ranges: the Pamirs in the west; the Tien Shan, Altai, and Ta Hingan in the north; and the Kunlun, Altyn Tagh, and Nan Shan in the south.

Back in the early 1600's, this vast, forbidding terrain was almost a complete mystery to Westerners. For 200 years, European access to the inland regions of China had been cut off by the combined might of the Chinese and the Moslems. Even after the Portuguese had reached the Orient by sea in the early 1500's, it was a full century before any Western traveler ventured into the heart of Central Asia. The man who eventually did so was, like the first explorers of Tibet, a brave Jesuit priest.

The Jesuits at Peking had long been at odds with their brethren in India over a perplexing geographical riddle: Where was Cathay? In the late 1200's, the great traveler Marco Polo had visited this Eastern realm and glowingly described it. But by the time the Portuguese arrived in the Orient, it seemed to have vanished into thin air. Matteo Ricci, head of the Jesuit mission at Peking, stoutly maintained that "Cathay" was simply an old name for China. This was true, and, in fact, some of China's land neighbors were still calling the Chinese empire "Cathay." But the Jesuits in India suspected that Marco Polo's fabled Asian realm was a different country from

Left: a detail from a Turkoman tent band, used to decorate the interior walls of the round tentlike structures that the Turkoman people lived in and carried with them on their travels. The design here is a caravan scene of men, horses, and camels.

Below: Matteo Ricci, who was the head of the Jesuit mission in Peking. He maintained that the mysterious "Cathay" was an old name for China.

China. To settle the issue once and for all, they decided to send an explorer deep into the Asian heartland to find Cathay.

The man they picked for this hazardous mission was a 41-year-old priest named Bento de Goes. He had started his career in India as a Portuguese soldier, and even after becoming a Jesuit—at the age of 26—had eagerly seized every opportunity for travel and adventure. De Goes was serving as the emissary of India's great Mogul ruler, Akbar, to the Portuguese viceroy at Goa when, in 1603, he received his orders to set out in search of Cathay.

After leaving Goa, De Goes traveled to the bustling city of Lahore, in present-day Pakistan. Knowing that he would be traveling through fanatically Moslem lands, he disguised himself as a Moslem merchant, and joined a large caravan bound for Kabul in eastern Afghanistan. The region between Lahore and Kabul was infested with bandits, and despite the size of the caravan—some 500 men with wagons, camels, and pack horses—an escort of 400 soldiers was necessary to get them through without too much loss of lives and property.

After six grueling months, the party reached Kabul, and there the Jesuit joined another caravan, this one bound for Yarkand (Soche) in Turkestan (now the Chinese province of Sinkiang-Uigur). Along the way, they had to cross the high, windswept passes of the Pamirs, and five of De Goes' seven horses died from the intense cold and the difficulty of breathing in the rarefied air. One day De Goes was cut off from the caravan by four bloodthirsty robbers. He managed to escape their clutches only by throwing his jeweled cap to the ground and galloping off while they fought for possession of it.

Left: an Indian miniature depicting the Mogul ruler Akbar with Jesuit missionaries. Akbar was much impressed by De Goes, who at one time became Akbar's ambassador to the Portuguese viceroy at Goa, under instructions to improve the strained relations between the Portuguese and the Indian court.

Above: Bento de Goes' caravan being set upon by bandits. The perils of travel were so well known that a small army had to travel with every large caravan to protect it from raiders.

Late in 1603, the caravan reached Yarkand, and De Goes settled down to wait for the departure of another large caravan which, he learned, was going to travel east "to Cathay." Shortly after his arrival in the city, he was almost murdered by an angry mob of Moslems who had seen through his disguise. At the last minute, the city's more tolerant ruler intervened, and placed the Jesuit under his protection. With the help of another local potentate, De Goes became the first European since Marco Polo to see the fabulous Khotan jade mines, 200 miles to the south.

Ready at last, the caravan set out in 1604 and began winding its way eastward along the foothills of the Tien Shan. Occasionally, it made stops at such obscure places as Aksu, Turfan, and Hami. At Aksu, De Goes was introduced to the king—a boy of 12—and gave him some sugar lumps. The boy was so delighted with this novel gift that he ordered a special dance in the traveler's honor. To please the king, De Goes danced too—much to the boy's amusement.

But such moments of gaiety were few and far between on the long road to China. In eastern Turkestan, there was the ever-present danger of a Mongol attack. De Goes recorded that passage through the region could be made only "in the greatest fear, sometimes even under cover of night, and in the strictest silence." The going got even rougher when they reached the outskirts of the Gobi Desert. There, all along the trail, lay the bleached bones of men and animals—grim reminders of the fate that awaited stragglers.

Late in 1605, the caravan reached its destination, a dusty trading station called Suchow, just north of the Nan Shan. De Goes learned from his traveling companions that this outpost marked the western-most limit of Cathay. So he had reached his objective! But had he also reached China? He put the question to a party of Peking merchants who arrived in Suchow a few days later. To his great joy, they assured him that he was indeed standing on Chinese soil.

Right: an engraving of the early 1700's, showing De Goes being poisoned by his fellow travelers. He lies dying in bed while the Moslems attack his servant and go through his papers. His diary was stolen, probably by men who wanted to remove all evidence of their indebtedness to De Goes. The only account of his journey comes from his servant, who managed to reach Ricci.

Left: the Gobi Desert. Covering vast areas in Mongolia and central China, the desert was a formidable buffer between China and the world to the west. Here the dangers of bandits receded in the face of the difficulties of finding a way across the arid waste.

Better still, one of the merchants happened to be a friend of Father Ricci, and offered to carry a letter to him from De Goes.

It took over a year for Ricci's answer to reach De Goes, and during that time the explorer was persecuted—and probably even poisoned—by his Moslem traveling companions. The priest was a dying man when, in March, 1607, he finally received Ricci's reply, urging him to proceed eastward through Cathay-China to Peking. But it was too late for De Goes. A few weeks later, the brave Jesuit died. "Seeking Cathay," one of his fellow priests wrote later, "he found heaven."

It was to be a long, long time before De Goes' harrowing journey was repeated by another European. In fact, the western half of Central Asia remained a blank on the map for another 200 years. In the meantime, however, a number of intrepid explorers made their way through the eastern deserts of the heartland.

The first of these daring travelers were, of course, the Jesuits Grueber and D'Orville, who journeyed from Peking to Agra in 1661–2. They were followed by a Dutch adventurer named Samuel van de Putte, who traveled from Europe to Peking—via Persia, India, and Tibet—*and back again*, in the 1720's and 1730's. But van de Putte was a strange man. He seemed not to want to tell anyone about his journey, and even burned his diaries before he died in 1745. All he left to the world as a record of his journey was a rough map of his route, and ironically, that, too, was later destroyed in a World War II bombing raid.

One of the first major scientific expeditions to Central Asia was led by the distinguished German geographer Alexander von Humboldt. In 1829, he traveled to the western edge of the Altai ranges on an expedition for the Russian government. But like van de Putte, the German was curiously modest about his exploits in the heartland. Having made his official report, he refrained from writing a personal account of his experiences in Central Asia.

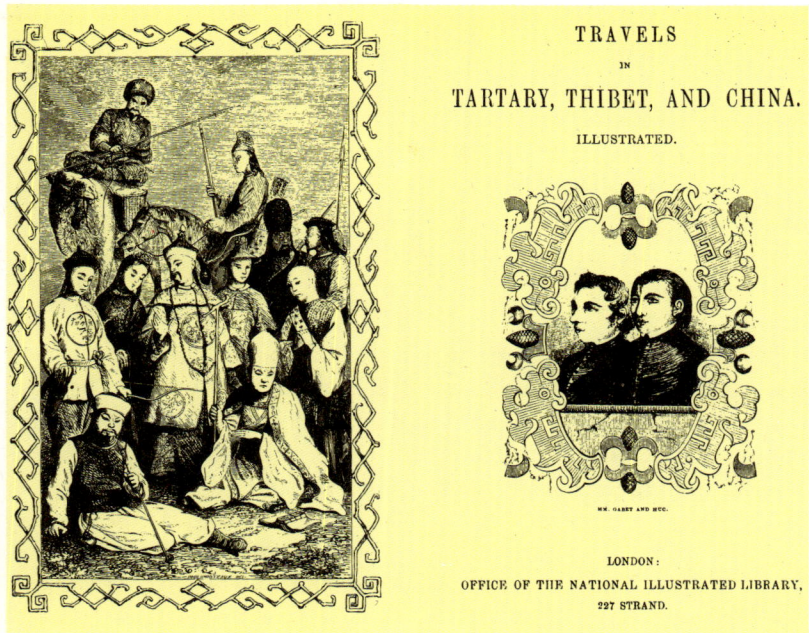

Left: the frontispiece and title page of Huc's account of his journey, *Travels in Tartary, Thibet, and China*. On the title page are pictured Huc and his traveling companion Gabet, and the frontispiece shows men in Mongol and Chinese dress, improbably grouped. Huc's story was so entertainingly told that for years few scholars believed it.

Modesty was definitely not a characteristic of a subsequent European traveler in the heartland. This was a French missionary named Father Evarist Huc, who, with a companion named Joseph Gabet, made an epic two-year tour of Mongolia, China, and Tibet in the mid-1800's. On his return, Huc published a long and colorful account of his travels—so colorful, in fact, that for years no one believed a word of it.

Huc and Gabet were working at a mission in northern China when they began their great adventure. They had had some success in converting the Buddhist Mongols of the Chinese interior, and decided to try their luck in Tibet. They knew it had been nearly 100 years since any missionaries had been allowed inside the country. But they hoped that by approaching Tibet from China, rather than from India, they would succeed where others had failed.

Having first disguised themselves as lamas—complete with shaven heads—the two set out from Yan-Pa-Eul, north of Peking, in 1844. They had decided to make a brief circuit through Tartary (Inner Mongolia), so they headed due north. Their route took them through a rugged, heavily forrested terrain which, they soon learned, was

Right: the interior of a Mongol tent, with the hole at the top to let out the smoke. Abbé Huc wrote about them, "The odor pervading the interior of the Mongol tents is, to those not accustomed to it, disgusting and almost insupportable. This smell, so potent sometimes that it seems to make one's heart rise to one's throat, is occasioned by the mutton grease and butter with which everything on or about a Tartar is impregnated."

notoriously infested with thieves. According to Huc, these bandits operated with a kind of sinister politeness. "Venerable elder brother," they would say as they held up a traveler, "I am on foot; pray lend me your horse." So saying, they would rob him of horse, money, and any other valuables he had with him, thanking him profusely all the while.

Huc and Gabet managed to get through this region safely, and proceeded west to the high plains of Tartary. Huc found the grasslands strangely beautiful. "The aspect of the prairies," he wrote,

"excites neither joy nor sorrow, but rather a mixture of the two, a sentiment of gentle, religious melancholy." These rolling plains were the home of the Mongol nomads, whose round felt tents looked from a distance "like balloons newly inflated and just about to take flight."

The missionaries found the nomads kindly and hospitable, and often stopped to rest with them. The scene at each camp was the same: "Children with a sort of hood at their backs run about collecting *argols* [dried dung used for fuel] which they pile in heaps

Below: a Mongol camp in the 1800's. The nomadic Mongols were completely at home in the steppes, being superb horsemen. They kept large herds of cattle and horses, and lived in tents—the famous Mongol *yurts*—that they could easily dismantle for traveling.

around their respective tents. The matrons look after the calves, make tea in the open air, or prepare milk in various ways. The men, mounted on fiery horses and armed with a long pole, gallop about, guiding to the best pastures the great herds of cattle which undulate in the distance all around like waves of the sea."

During their sojourn among the Mongols, Huc recorded many of their customs and beliefs. One of these—a tradition that horrified the missionary—was their practice of supplying dead kings with slaves. Just before the tomb was sealed, the Mongols "take children of both sexes remarkable for their beauty, and make them swallow mercury until they are suffocated. In this way they preserve the freshness and ruddiness of their countenances so as to make them appear still alive." The Mongols placed these unfortunate children in the tomb together with the king, in the belief that they would serve him in the afterlife.

Huc and Gabet traveled some 300 miles through forests and prairies before entering the bleak wastes of the Ordos Desert.

Right: Mongol herdsmen of today, little changed from the Mongols abbé Huc described, riding horses and using long poles to guide their herds.

There, Nature inspired no sentiments of "religious melancholy." The Ordos was more like a giant enemy armed with a variety of fiendish weapons. It was the middle of winter, and the missionaries found the nights almost unbearably cold. During the day, fierce winds often drove blinding clouds of sand into the eyes of the men and their camels. But worst of all were the frequent hailstorms. Like everything else about this desert, the hailstones were Gargantuan—rocks of ice as big as a fist.

The only refuge from the elements was the occasional *serai*, or

Above: an engraving from the English edition of Huc's book showing the Tree of Ten Thousand Images. Huc wrote, "More profound intellects than ours may, perhaps, be able to supply a satisfactory explanation of the mysteries of this singular tree; but as to us, we altogether give it up."

desert inn. These welcome havens were no more than rough huts, but they offered warmth, shelter, and companionship to weary travelers after a long day's march in the desert. At such waystations, Huc and Gabet would join caravan merchants around long furnaces called *kangs*, smoking, swapping stories, and philosophizing far into the night.

Twice during their journey westward, the missionaries had to cross the great Hwang Ho. The first time, the river was in flood, and proved a formidable obstacle. The camels could not swim, and had to be ferried in small, unstable craft across the swirling waters. But at the second crossing, the travelers encountered no difficulty and left the Ordos Desert behind them. Early in 1845, after "ascending many hills and twice passing the Great Wall," Huc and Gabet reached Kumbum, a Buddhist sanctuary near the Koko Nor. There the missionaries made the acquaintance of a learned lama, and gained his permission to enter the famous Kumbum lamasery.

Kumbum was the sacred birthplace of Tsong Khapa, a great Buddhist teacher of the 1300's. Tsong Khapa had become a lama at the age of three, and legend has it that when his shorn locks were thrown on the ground, a miraculous tree sprang up. On each one of its leaves was a character of the sacred Tibetan language.

Huc and Gabet, who spent several months at the Kumbum lamasery, were convinced of the genuineness of this "Tree of Ten Thousand Images." Huc wrote that "We were filled with an absolute consternation of astonishment at finding that there were upon each of these leaves well-formed Tibetan characters, all of a green character." The two men examined the tree minutely, and found that "when you remove a piece of the old bark, the young bark under it exhibits the indistinct outlines of characters in a germinating state."

For two devout Catholic priests to acknowledge a "heathen" miracle was practically a miracle in itself. Yet they had the evidence before their very eyes. Was it genuine? We shall never know, for by the time the next European traveler reached Kumbum, 50 years later, the miraculous tree had died.

The Kumbum lamasery was both a shrine and a medical center. Huc watched the lama-physicians at work, and describes how they would diagnose a patient's illness by listening to a sample of his urine, "to ascertain how much noise it makes; for in their view a

...lise for sale in Peking. When we met the first ...l-driver, we asked him how far it was from ...e Enclosure. "You see here," said he with a

grin, "one end of our caravan; the other extremity is still within the town." "Thanks," cried we; "in that case we shall soon be there." "Well, you've not more than fifteen lis to go." "Fifteen lis! why you've just told us that the other end of your caravan is still in the town." "So it is, but our

Above: a page from Huc's book showing one of the immense caravans he and Gabet had seen. This particular one was on its way to Lhasa from Peking.

Right: a drawing of the Potala at Lhasa in crayon, showing it as it looked in 1904. Huc, like those who came to the city before him, was much impressed by its magnificence.

The Pota-la Palace: Lhasa

patient's water is mute or silent according to the state of his health." The missionary also watched the lamas making the herbal medicines for which Kumbum was famous. "The Tartar-Mongols never return home without an ample supply of them, having an unlimited confidence in whatever emanates from Kumbum, even though the very same roots and grasses grow in abundance in their own lands."

At the end of October, 1845, a large caravan from Peking passed near Kumbum on its way to Lhasa. Here was a golden opportunity, and the two priests were quick to take advantage of it. When they joined the caravan, their presence was hardly noticed amid the throng of 2,000 men and 5,000 animals that made up the entourage.

The long column of men and beasts slowly made its way south over the high rim of mountains guarding the Tibetan plateau. Winter was setting in, and the wind cut through them like a knife as they stumbled along through deep drifts of snow. To keep from losing their way in blizzards, the men walked behind their horses, holding on to their tails and trusting to their instinct. "Death now hovered over the unfortunate caravan," writes Huc. "Each day we had to abandon beasts of burden that could drag themselves no further. The turn of the men came somewhat later. . . ." But still the caravan pressed on, and at long last, on January 29, 1846, the travelers reached Lhasa.

Like Grueber and Desideri before him, Huc was deeply impressed by the Potala palace. "Two fine avenues of magnificent trees lead from Lhasa to the Buddha-la [Potala], and there you always find crowds of foreign pilgrims. . . . The Potala inspires a strange silence." But the atmosphere in the city itself was very different. In the streets, "all is excitement and noise and pushing . . . every single soul in the place being ardently occupied in the business of buying and selling."

The missionaries' arrival in the "holy city" created a sensation. Word went round that they were foreign spies, and they were summoned to the palace for a confrontation with the reigning regent. For a long time, the regent stared silently at the two men before him. Finally, just the hint of a smile on the man's face prompted Huc to whisper to Gabet, "This gentleman seems a good fellow." The regent immediately wanted to know what he had said, so Huc repeated his remark in Tibetan. At this, the regent burst out laughing, for in truth, he said, he was really bad-tempered. But the ice had been broken, and thereafter, the ruler often invited Huc and Gabet to the palace to discuss religion and tell him about the outside world.

One day, the regent asked Huc to show him the microscope that the missionary had brought with him from Peking. The Tibetan wanted to know how it worked. Accordingly, writes Huc, "We asked if one of the company would be so good as to produce us a louse. A lama had merely to put his hand under his silk dress to his armpit, and an extremely vigorous louse was at our disposal. . . . We requested the regent to apply his right eye, shutting his left, to the glass top of the machine. 'Tsong Khapa!' exclaimed the regent, 'The louse is as big as a rat!'"

The priests' friendship with the regent led them to hope that sooner or later they would succeed in converting him to Catholicism. And if he became a Christian, who could tell how many other Tibetans might follow suit? But it was not to be. Two months after their arrival, the resident Chinese ambassador—who had been suspicious of them from the start—ordered them to leave Tibet.

The regent was genuinely sorry to see them go, and provided them with a military escort to ensure their safe return to Peking.

Left: the regent of Lhasa, shown with pen in hand. Huc said of his writing that he was not able to judge of its literary merit, but that he had never seen such beautiful calligraphy.

Below: two Ladakh lamas blowing their beautiful ceremonial long brass horns. Often the only sounds Tibetan travelers hear are the wind and the eerie traditional music of these horns.

The Tibetans helped them find a shorter and easier route back, and by June, 1846, the missionaries were once again on the warm plains of eastern China. They had not succeeded in converting Tibet, but they had penetrated Tibet from China which had not been done by any European since Samuel van de Putte, 120 years before.

Huc and Gabet were the last of the great Catholic missionary explorers to venture into Tibet. From 1850 onward, the Asian interior increasingly became the haunt of explorers with a more worldly end in view. This was particularly true of the explorers in northern India and the Himalaya. There, in the region first penetrated by the Jesuits, a wave of British merchants, surveyors, and military officers had already begun writing a spectacular new chapter in the history of Asian exploration.

Penetrating the Himalaya
6

In May, 1774, a young Scotsman named George Bogle set out from northeast India on a crucial diplomatic mission. His task was nothing less than to gain access to Tibet, to learn all that he could about it, and to persuade its rulers to open their gates to the British.

Why were the British interested in Tibet? The answer lies in their phenomenal rise to power on the subcontinent below it. As far back as the early 1600's, English merchants of the East India Company had won powerful trading concessions in India. Year by year, the company had grown in wealth and power, aggressively extending its sphere of influence by scooping up hundreds of tiny Indian states. So successful were its political intrigues—and outright

conquests—that by the late 1700's, the East India Company was virtually master of India.

With almost the whole of the subcontinent in its pocket, the company naturally began to look beyond India's frontiers, to the remote Himalayan kingdoms. Tibet in particular intrigued the British. What trading opportunities did it offer? How close were its ties with China? Would it consider a trade alliance with Britain?

These were just some of the questions that George Bogle was to answer on his Himalayan mission. It was a tough assignment, for as yet no Englishman had penetrated beyond Nepal and Bhutan. Little was known about the Tibetan terrain—and still less about Tibetan

Above left: the East India Company had gradually gained wealth and power in India until, in the late 1700's it virtually controlled the subcontinent. In about 1790 the chess set from which these pieces are taken was carved of ivory in Bengal, and depicts the East India Company men pitted against the soldiers of an Indian army.

Above: Warren Hastings, the governor of Bengal who sent George Bogle off to establish contact with Tibet, and hopefully to persuade the Tibetans to permit the British to trade with them.

politics. But Bogle was a daring and cool-headed young man, and Warren Hastings, the company's governor of Bengal, was confident that he would make the right decisions whatever happened.

Bogle almost failed to get into Tibet. On the very borders of the kingdom, he was turned back by an emissary from the Panchen Lama—Tibet's second most powerful Buddhist leader—who strongly urged him to return to India. But Bogle was not ready to give up. He began a lively correspondence with the lama, petitioning him for a special audience. At last, his persistence paid off. In September, 1774, he received permission to visit the Panchen Lama at his temporary residence at Dsheripgay near Shigatse.

No European had seen the lamasery of Dsheripgay where the Panchen Lama had moved three years earlier because of a smallpox epidemic in Shigatse. Bogle's arrival caused a sensation. Crowds of people came running out to watch as he walked slowly through the streets to the lamasery. He wondered how he would be received by the Panchen Lama. But he found the great man astonishingly open and kindly. Within several days, the two were talking like old friends. They discussed the purpose of Bogle's mission, and soon came to an agreement about British trade with Tibet. The agreement, however, could not be put into practice without the consent of the Lhasa authorities. And it would take some careful negotiating, the lama assured Bogle, to get their approval.

In fact, Bogle was to wait five months in the palaces of the Panchen Lama before leaving. But it was a time of fascinating experiences in a world unlike anything Bogle had ever known. Soon after his arrival, the Panchen Lama moved to a much grander lamasery at Tashilhumpo. Hundreds of high-ranking priests came from all over to pay homage to the lama at his new quarters, and a great banquet was held. Bogle and the other guests dined on such strange delicacies as dried sheep's carcasses and tea buttered with yak fat. While they ate, they were entertained by scores of brightly garbed dancers who performed "to the music of flutes, kettledrums, and bells, keeping time with hoppings and twirlings."

Above: a watercolor by Lieutenant Samuel Davis who accompanied Turner on the journey to Tibet. The drawing shows a scene in Bhutan, with the mountain tops covered with clouds.

Left: the Director's Court Room of the East India House in Leadenhall Street, London. From this room the decision went out that the Company should try to make contact with the rulers of Tibet, as the area showed promise as a new market for goods from England.

Right: George Bogle, who managed to reach Tibet and became a friend of the Panchen Lama. When he set out he was only 28 years old.

Bogle's own quarters consisted of a dim monastery hall supported by nine square pillars painted red and white. There he was visited by a seemingly endless procession of curious Tibetans who came to stare at him as though he were an animal in a zoo. On his side, Bogle was amazed at the filthiness of the Tibetans' hands and faces. "It is directly contrary to custom for the inhabitants, whether male or female, high or low, ever to wash," he wrote. He did his best to interest Tibetans in washing, but met with little success. One day, Bogle's Tibetan servant happened to come in while he was shaving. "I prevailed on him," writes Bogle, "for once to scrub himself with the help of soap and water. I gave him a new complexion, and he seemed to view himself in my shaving glass with some satisfaction. But he was exposed to so much ridicule . . . that I could never get him to repeat the experiment!"

Left: a young Incarnate Lama of the
Yellow Hat sect. He is a 17th incarnate,
a lama of Kye monastery in Spiti on the
border of Tibet and Ladakh. Tibetans
believe that when a great lama dies, his
soul is reborn in another body, and
a search is undertaken for auspicious
signs that will direct the remaining
lamas to their reborn leader. When
Turner was there the new Panchen
Lama was only 18 months old.

Bogle whiled away his days at Tashilhumpo playing chess with
the monks and writing a history of Europe for his friend the Panchen
Lama. Over the months he became increasingly fond of the Lama.
"He is extremely merry and entertaining in conversations," Bogle
wrote, "and so universally beloved . . . that not a man could find in
his heart to speak ill of him."

The young Scotsman was equally enchanted by one of the Lama's
pretty young cousins. He married her, and later took her back to
India with him. His family, horrified at this exotic alliance, tried
to suppress the fact after his death. But we do know that Bogle and
his Tibetan wife had two daughters, both of whom were later
brought up in Scotland.

All during his stay at Tashilhumpo, Bogle hoped that Lhasa would
ultimately agree to the trade arrangements he had worked out with
the Panchen Lama. But it never came through. The Dalai Lama's
regent refused to sanction it, no doubt at the Chinese ambassador's
insistence. After all, it was in China's best interests to keep any other
foreign influences out of the kingdom.

At last, Bogle was forced to give up and return to India. The
Panchen Lama bade him a sad farewell, throwing a ceremonial
white scarf around his neck and gently laying his hand upon his
head in a last blessing. Six years later, both men were dead, struck
down suddenly by illness within six months of each other.

The East India Company made no further attempts to negotiate
with Tibet until 1783, when Warren Hastings sent another young
envoy to Tashilhumpo. This envoy, Samuel Turner, was no more
successful than Bogle in gaining trade concessions for the British.
But he did meet the new Panchen Lama. Like the Dalai Lama, the
new potentate of Tashilhumpo was chosen by divine signs, and
Turner found himself confronting an 18-month-old child. But
however skeptical he might have been before he met the boy, he
came away profoundly impressed by his apparent wisdom. Seated
on a high pile of cushions, the child listened attentively to all that
Turner said and, "while unable to speak . . . made the most expressive
signs and conducted himself with astonishing dignity and decorum."

Whatever faint hopes the British still had for establishing trade
links with Tibet were finally extinguished in 1792. In that year,
the East India Company's new governor general, Charles Cornwallis,
made a grave tactical error. He received a desperate letter from the

Above: Charles Cornwallis, governor
general of the East India Company. One
result of his refusal to help the Tibetans
when they were invaded by Nepalese
forces was that Tibet closed its doors
to all British explorers.

Panchen Lama's regent begging for the company's help against a Nepalese army that was heading for Tashilhumpo. Warren Hastings would have leapt at this chance to "save Tibet" and thereby win a British foothold in the kingdom. But Cornwallis was a cautious man. He decided not to risk company soldiers so far from India.

As a result, Tibet had to turn to China for assistance. A massive Chinese army arrived in 1792, swept away the Nepalese invaders, and placed Tibet under its "protection." Thereafter, Tibet remained under Chinese suzerainty for 120 years.

Another consequence of Cornwallis' decision was that the Tibetans began to regard the British as treacherous. As far as they were concerned, the East India Company had proved itself a false friend. Tibet officially closed its gates to the British, and became more of a forbidden land than ever. During the whole of the 1800's, only one Englishman was to gain access to Lhasa—and he was so eccentric that his exploits were not taken seriously.

This odd and unsung hero was Thomas Manning. For some years he had been devoured by curiosity about the exotic lands of Tartary. In 1806, his dream of visiting them came true when he won an appointment to the East India Company's offices in China. But this only increased his wanderlust, and in 1810, he turned up at Calcutta and asked if he might serve as the company's representative to Lhasa. The British officials refused his petition, and laughed at him behind his back. How could this bizarre person, sporting a long flowing beard and exotic "Tartary" robes, be expected to achieve anything significant?

But achieve it he did. In December, 1811, four months after leaving Calcutta, Thomas Manning became the first Englishman to enter Lhasa. How did he accomplish this remarkable feat? His diary offers few details about the journey itself. Mostly it is full of complaints about his rascally Chinese servant, and the occasional quip about Tibetan peculiarities. On seeing a long funeral procession carrying a corpse to the top of a hill for the vultures to feed on, Manning remarked, "The people of Tibet eat no birds . . . on the contrary, they let the birds eat them!"

While still some distance from Lhasa, Manning made the acquaintance of a Chinese general. Right away, he won the general's favor with a gift of two bottles of cherry brandy. This act was in return for the general's "promise to write immediately to the

Left: Thomas Manning, the casual and unsponsored explorer who became the first Englishman to reach Lhasa, in 1811. He was a brilliant but eccentric man who had long been fascinated by China and the mysterious land of Tibet.

Below: a watercolor by Hyder Young Hearsey of three Tibetan musicians at Ghertope, in the western sector of Tibet. Hearsey and his companion William Moorcroft traveled there in 1812 disguised as Indian holy men.

Lhasa Mandarin [Chinese ambassador] for permission for me to proceed."

Once in Lhasa, Manning went to visit the seven-year-old Dalai Lama. He was deeply moved by the interview and wrote in his diary, "This day I saluted the Grand Lama! Beautiful youth. Face poetically affecting. Very happy to have seen him and his blessed smile. Hope often to see him again." Whether he did or not is not clear. From then on, Manning's diary mentions his growing fear of the sinister Chinese officials in the city. They kept him under constant surveillance and made it pointedly clear that he was not

welcome. At last, in April, 1812, Manning took the hint and left the city. By June he was back in India recounting his adventures to the open-mouthed officials of the East India Company.

The very year Manning returned from Lhasa, two young company officers named Moorcroft and Hearsey became the first Englishmen to explore the interior of western Tibet. Dressed as Indian *fakirs* (holy men), they made their way deep into the Himalaya and brought back new and valuable geographical data about Nepal's northwestern mountain ranges and the Lake Manasarowar region of Tibet.

Since the late 1700's, the British had been engaged in a scientific survey of the Indian subcontinent, and in 1818 these efforts became known as "The Great Trigonometrical Survey". Not only was the subcontinent to be surveyed, but also the 2,000-mile arc of mountains beyond it. An accurate map of India and the Himalayan kingdoms north of it was essential if the British were to maintain and extend their Indian empire.

But getting the information—particularly in the jagged mountains of northern India, Kashmir, and Nepal—was often difficult and dangerous. There the surveyors had to contend with hostile tribesmen, as well as with all the perils and hardships of mountain travel. But the work went on, and by 1863 most of the region south and west of Tibet had been accurately mapped. Not the least of the surveyors' achievements was to calculate the height of the world's loftiest peak, Mount Everest, on the Nepal-Tibet border.

But Tibet itself remained an enigma. As the years went by, the Tibetan authorities increased their vigilance, and it became impossible for British surveyors—no matter how well disguised—to gain access to the country. This was doubly frustrating because knowledge of Tibet had assumed a momentous strategic importance. Beyond it lay the powerful empires of Russia and China. Edgy about the security of their Indian holdings, the British were anxious to learn all they could about the mountain fortress that guarded the northern approaches to the subcontinent. But how were they to do so if the Tibetans would not let them enter their kingdom?

It was a surveyor named T. G. Montgomerie who found the solution. He hit upon the idea of training Indians to carry out a secret survey of Tibet. Traveling in the guise of merchants or pilgrims, such native explorers could enter the forbidden land and obtain the vital information needed to fill the blanks on the map.

The Indians chosen for this important task were given an intensive course of training in the use of various surveying instruments, as well as in the techniques of navigational astronomy. But scientific method was not the only thing these "pundit-explorers" learned. Because, in effect, they were British spies, they were taught a variety of ingenious techniques to conceal their real identity and purpose. They were given code names, clothes with secret pockets, and Tibetan prayer wheels with hidden compartments for storing notes. They were encouraged to memorize important information in the form of cryptic verses, and taught special methods of measuring distance, using prayer beads as counting markers and regulating their stride so that each step could be counted as a unit of measure.

All these clandestine techniques were used to great effect by a remarkable pundit named Nain Singh. Traveling as a Tibetan trader, he journeyed through Nepal, and reached Tashilhumpo late in 1865. From there, he traveled east to Lhasa. Soon after his arrival in the city, some resident merchants saw through his disguise, but for reasons best known to themselves, decided not to inform the authorities. Nain Singh kept off the streets as much as possible, and carried out his survey in the strictest secrecy. Working at night from the roof of his humble accommodation, he made a series of astronomical observations that enabled him to plot the exact location of Lhasa for the first time in history.

From Lhasa, Nain Singh journeyed to Tibet's sacred Lake Manasarowar, just beyond the northwest corner of Nepal, and then returned to India. In all, he had covered some 1,200 miles—each of them laboriously measured in footsteps—and obtained crucial information about Tibet's southern trade routes. On his next mission, in 1867, he explored western Tibet, and visited the fabled Thok-Jalung gold mines. There, at an encampment guarded by fierce Tibetan mastiffs, he saw a group of black-clad workers digging out lumps of gold as much as two pounds in weight. He noted that they only mined the surface of the soil, because they believed that to dig for gold deep underground would rob the soil of its fertility.

The next great pundit-explorer was Kishen Singh. In 1878 he made his way to Lhasa, and joined a caravan of Tibetan and Mongolian merchants bound for Chinese Turkestan. His object was to make a thorough survey of the route north, but it was an immensely difficult task. All the while he was making his observations, he had

Bogle		1	1774-5
Turner		2	1783-4
Manning		3	1811-2
Hearsey		4a	1808
Hearsey (with Moorcroft)		4b	1812
Moorcroft		5	1819-25
Nain Singh (part with Main Singh)		6a	1865-6
Nain Singh (with Main Singh & Kalian Singh)		6b	1867
Nain Singh (with Kishen Singh)		6c	1874
Nain Singh		6d	1874-5
Kishen Singh		7a	1869
Kishen Singh		7b	1871-2
Kishen Singh (with Nain Singh)		7c	1873-4
Kishen Singh		7d	1878-82
Kintup (K.P.)		8	1879-83

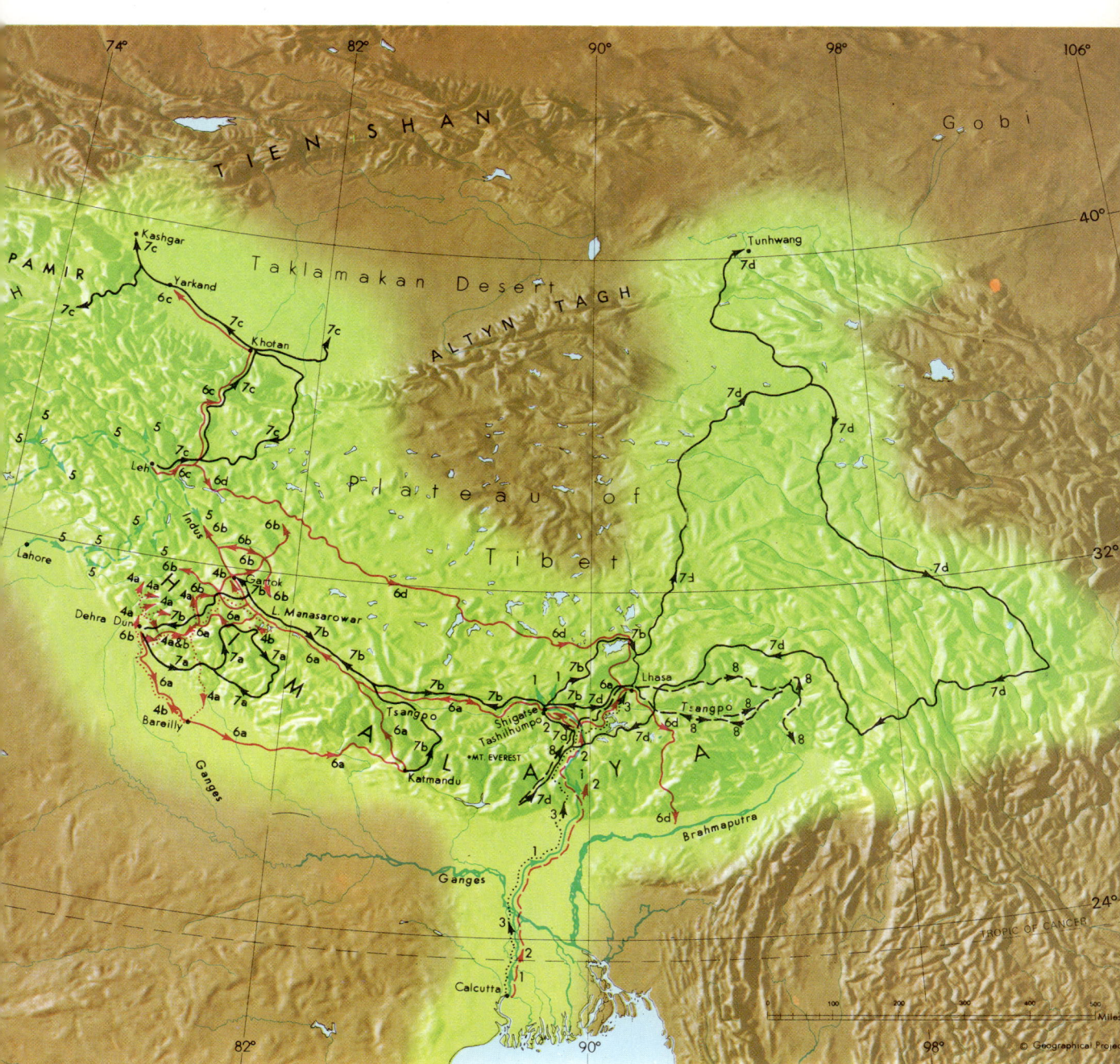

Above: a portrait of Nain Singh, one of the earliest and most famous of all the pundits. His training lasted for two years, during which time he became expert in the use of the compass and sextant, and learned to measure his steps so that every pace was exactly uniform for calculating distances.

to keep up the pretense that he was just a simple merchant who happened to enjoy star-gazing. Fortunately, he was able to travel on foot, so he was able to measure distances fairly accurately. But on one occasion, the caravan leader insisted that they ride horses to speed up their journey through a bandit-infested area. Undaunted, the pundit "set at once to work counting the beast's paces," reckoning the distance in this way for almost 230 miles.

Kishen Singh traveled all the way to Tunhwang, at the western end of the Gobi Desert. He then made his way back to Tibet, visiting most of the principal towns in the eastern sector. He finally returned to India in 1882, after a remarkable journey of several thousand miles through hitherto unknown territories.

Another four-year Tibetan odyssey was made by a dogged native of Sikkim named Kintup—or K.P., as he was known in the survey code. In 1880, he set out for the Tsangpo River in southern Tibet as a servant of a Mongolian lama, who had been commissioned by the India Survey Department to lead the expedition. The department's confidence in the lama soon proved to be misplaced. Kintup's Mongolian master sold him to a Tibetan lama, who kept him under almost constant surveillance. It was only after six months of bondage that Kintup managed to make his escape. But despite the

indignities he had suffered, Kintup was determined to complete his mission. He set off for the Tsangpo and after following unexplored portions of the river, he returned to India in 1884.

The work of Nain Singh, Kishen Singh, and Kintup—together with that of many other, lesser known, pundits—contributed immeasurably to the knowledge of the mysterious lands northeast of India. Meanwhile, to the northwest, British surveyors and explorers were hard at work mapping the strategic territory between India and the exotic land of Persia.

Right: K.P., the explorer Kintup, who doggedly stuck to his task in spite of a series of mishaps and difficulties. His mission was to reach the Tsangpo so that its relationship with the Brahmaputra River of India might be determined. He was enslaved, but managed to escape and eventually completed his mission.

Left: a small pocket sextant, made in England in about 1790, of the type that the pundits would have used. They were taught to remember their notes by transcribing them into verse and constantly reciting them as they walked, as pilgrims did the Buddhist prayers.

Above: a detail from a painting of the court of Fath Ali, shah of Persia, in the early 1800's, showing all the foreign ambassadors who had suddenly surged into Persia. Sir John Malcolm is the figure in European dress nearest to the king on his righthand side.

Far right: the imposing portrait of Fath Ali with his magnificent full beard and jewel-encrusted robes. He reigned as shah from 1797 to 1834.

Persia and the "Great Game"

7

During the late 1700's, while the British were building up their vast Indian empire, they all but forgot about Persia. Ravaged and impoverished by civil war, the kingdom had long since lost its appeal for British merchants. And in any case, why should they bother with this dusty corner of Asia when the riches of India lay at their feet? In fact, the British might well have gone on ignoring Persia, had it not suddenly become vital to the security of India itself.

In earlier times, Persia had been famous as a "gateway to the East." In 1798, that phrase abruptly took on a new and sinister meaning for the British. Word had reached them that Napoleon was eying the kingdom as a possible gateway to India. Already, the French army had invaded Egypt and established its influence around the eastern Mediterranean Sea. Further conquests in the Middle East would place Persia within reach of the conqueror's army. It was also known that Russian power was slowly extending through the Caucasus, the region between the Black and Caspian seas, toward Persia. Thoroughly alarmed by these possibilities, the British decided that it was high time they established their own sphere of influence in Persia.

The man picked to spearhead this move was a young officer in the East India Company's army, Captain John Malcolm. Armed with gifts for the shah, he traveled by ship from Bombay to the Persian Gulf, and then he set off for the new Persian capital of Teheran. When

he reached the city, late in 1800, he found himself the object of wonder and suspicion. It was hardly surprising, because many, many years had passed since any European had sought an audience with the shah. The Persian officials, being sticklers for etiquette, asked that Malcolm dress like the Englishmen who had visited the kingdom in the 1600's. They had seen a painting of Sir Anthony Sherley, and expected Malcolm to copy the old styles of dress for his presentation to the shah. Malcolm refused to comply with this as he believed it would lower the shah's esteem for him.

Powerful and persuasive, Malcolm soon won the confidence of the shah, Fath Ali, and convinced him that it would be in his best interests to ally himself with the British. Then, playing on the shah's fear of foreign invasion, Malcolm promised to send British military equipment and ammunition should Persia be attacked. In return, the shah agreed to bring pressure on the Afghan ruler to make peace with the British in India.

Over the next 10 years, two more visits by Malcolm and one by another envoy, Sir Harford Jones Brydges, clinched this new friendship between Britain and Persia. A permanent British embassy was set up in Teheran, and soldiers that Brydges promised duly arrived. However, to the dismay of the British, even the expert advice of these officers could not prevent the shah's army from losing ground to the Russians.

Above: a Persian miniature showing a battle between the Persian and Russian armies. Fath Ali is shown leading the Persian forces to victory, although on most of the occasions when the Persians fought the Russians, it was the czar's armies who won the day.

Hopelessly undisciplined, the Persian troops did not know how to seize the advantage even when they had it. On one occasion, with victory practically in sight, the Persian commander suddenly lost his head, gave a series of wildly contradictory orders, and ended by calling a retreat. Another time, when the Persians had actually won a battle, they wasted so much time cutting off the heads of a few captives that they let the main body of the enemy force escape.

Part of the trouble lay with the shah himself. Fath Ali was an incorrigibly selfish man, and he simply could not be persuaded to spend money on equipment for his army. Worse still, he seemed to be unaware of just how serious the situation was. His reaction to the news of one particularly crushing defeat was to appear before his courtiers dressed all in red. Fantastic as it may seem, he imagined

that word of his wearing his "robes of wrath" would reach the Russians and frighten them off!

Fortunately, the Russians ceased their attacks on Persia in 1828. For the moment, they were content with the strategic gains they had made along the southeastern shores of the Caspian Sea. But the end of the conflict by no means marked the end of British fears. Persia was now under Russia's thumb in some respects, and there was a powerful Russian embassy in Teheran. Countering Russian influence in Persia became a full-time job for British diplomats.

As a result of this renewed interest in Persia, European merchants and travelers were lured back to the country. Among these travelers was the artist Robert Ker Porter, who journeyed to Persia to paint and sketch in 1817. After passing through Teheran, Porter stopped at

Above: a watercolor of Persia by Robert Ker Porter, here the View of Guz Kala and the Pass of the Koflan-Kou Mountains. Ker Porter writes that the road to the pass was steep, winding, intricate, and very dangerous because of the slipperiness of the ice surface.

Above: Fath Ali receiving Sir Harford Jones Brydges in 1809. The painting is possibly by James Morier, shown standing behind the ambassador. He took part in three missions to Persia.

Right: James Morier's diaries. The one opened describes a visit to a Russian camp in October, 1813, and the incident is illustrated by a watercolor sketch. Many travelers of the 1800's and 1900's kept detailed diaries.

the fabled city of Isfahan. Alas, the city had lost much of its splendor since the days of Shah Abbas. Years of war and neglect had turned Isfahan into a waste of ruins and abandoned houses. Though it was still inhabited, Porter recorded sadly that "its palaces [are] solitary and forlorn. . . . The nocturnal laugh and song which used to echo from every part of the gardens [are] now succeeded by the yells of jackalls and the howls of famishing dogs."

And what of the new Persian capital, Teheran? Set at the very foot of the snow-clad Elburz Mountains, the city looked from a distance every bit as romantic as European tourists expected it to be. But once inside its gates, they found to their astonishment that the capital was little more than a squalid, overgrown market town, a hodgepodge of low, flat-roofed houses and crowded bazaars.

James Morier, a British diplomat who spent many years in Teheran, vividly captured the typical European's first impressions of this strange city. "In vain he looks for a street. . . . He makes his way through the narrowest lanes, incumbered with filth, dead animals, and mangy dogs. He hears a language totally new . . . spoken by people whose looks and dress are equally extraordinary—rough faces masked with beards and moustachios, in long flapping clothes . . . . At dawn the *muezzins* [Moslem criers] are heard in a great variety of tones, calling the people to prayer from the top of the mosques; these are mixed with the sounds of cow horns . . . to inform the women, who bathe before the men . . . that the *hummums* [public baths] are ready. The cow horns set all the dogs to barking in a frightful manner. The asses of the town generally begin to bray about the same time. . . ."

James Morier, like most British visitors to Persia in the early 1800's, found little to praise in the country. But Morier spiced his criticisms with wit. One of his most amusing—and uncomplimentary—books about life in Persia was a satire called *Hajji Baba*. It describes the adventures of a young man, the Hajji Baba of the title, as he passes through a wild variety of careers—as a slave, a dervish, an executioner, a holy man, a scribe, a tobacco dealer, and finally an assistant to an ambassador. Morier was a shrewd observer, and the

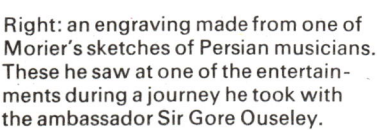

Right: an engraving made from one of Morier's sketches of Persian musicians. These he saw at one of the entertainments during a journey he took with the ambassador Sir Gore Ouseley.

Left: a harem lady tumbling, in an oil painting of the early 1800's, from the shah's palace. The strange position of the lady shows clearly her voluminous trousers. The more noble a woman was, the more layers of trousers she wore. When Lady Shiel first appeared wearing a dress she caused a great flurry as the Persians thought she was wearing trousers with only one leg.

fictional characters in the story were, in fact, only thinly disguised versions of real people. The ambassador in the tale, for example, was based on the Persian envoy whom Morier himself had accompanied to London in 1809.

This ambassador, a man named Mirza Abul Hassan, was so outraged when he read the book that he sat down and wrote Morier an angry letter. "What for you write Hajji Baba, sir?" he demanded. "That very bad book, sir. All lies, sir. Who tell you these lies, sir? What for you not speak to me? Very bad business, sir. Persian people very bad people, perhaps, but very good to you, sir. What for you abuse them so bad?"

But there was a good deal of truth in Morier's account. Persia at this time was rife with corruption and governmental abuses. Extortion was the rule all the way up the ladder of authority, and the shah maintained his tyrannical grip over the country with arbitrary acts of extreme cruelty. Lady Shiel, the wife of a British ambassador in Persia in the mid-1800's, recounts how the shah used to levy a fine in the form of eyes from those cities that incurred his displeasure. The eyes had to be brought to him on a platter, and he would count them, in the presence of all his courtiers, with the tip of his jeweled sword. On one occasion, no less than 70,000 pairs of eyes were exacted from the province of Kerman as a punishment for sheltering a rival prince.

Rival princes abounded, for by the 1800's, it was common for the shah to have literally hundreds of sons. James Morier recorded that on a single night in 1808, the shah, who already had 65 sons, was presented with another four sons and two daughters. And when Lady Shiel visited the country, 30 years later, she was astonished to discover that the shah's "family" included some 2,500 people! Most of the shah's children lived at the royal palace as his dependants. But some of the princes were permitted to take charge of distant provinces. If and when they acquired too much power and began to intrigue against their father, they were promptly killed or blinded.

The shah stocked his harem with beautiful women from all over Persia. Government officials used to roam the kingdom seeking pretty virgins to please the king, and Persian nobles were expected to offer their wives to him as potential mistresses. All the women in the royal harem were kept in strict seclusion, under the care of a man

Above: a papier-mâché Persian pen box, decorated with the picture of the court of a eunuch who had become a governor. The shah put the royal princes in the care of the eunuchs in the harem to keep them uninvolved in the world of politics and therefore less of a threat to his own position.

Below: a watercolor drawing by Robert Ker Porter of one of the harem women. He wrote that their personal beauty seldom lasted longer than eight or ten years, and then faded quickly.

called a eunuch, who could be trusted because he had been castrated.

The keeping of women in seclusion—or *purdah*, as it was called—was standard practice throughout Persia. A woman was allowed to be seen only by her family. If she ventured out of the house, she had to wear a *bourkha,* a tent-like garment that covered her from head to toe. While in Persia, Lady Shiel was forced to adopt this garb lest she be thought indecent. She resented the custom at first, but later came to the conclusion that it gave Persian women a freedom and anonymity their British sisters might well envy. Hidden under the folds of their bourkhas, they could travel incognito wherever they wanted.

In spite of the interest she took in Persian customs, however, Lady Shiel found life in Persia very dull. There was only one other educated European woman in Teheran, and she was the wife of the Russian minister. Since their husbands were political enemies, it was impossible for the two women to become friends. Lady Shiel occasionally accompanied her husband on diplomatic missions to other parts of the country, but these journeys could hardly be described as pleasure trips. As she herself put it, Persia was divided into "two portions—one being desert with salt, and the other desert without salt." Nor was the Persian climate endearing. The winters were extremely cold, and often accompanied by severe blizzards. In summer, the whole country baked in a sweltering heat so intense that "ivory split, mathematical rulers curled up, and the mercury overran the boxes which contained it."

But if life in Persia was dull for diplomats' wives, it was frustrating and difficult for the diplomats themselves—particularly during the second half of the 1800's. Shah Nasiru'd Din, who ruled from 1848 to 1896, stubbornly refused to commit himself to either the British

Left: Abdel Samud, the Afghan official responsible for having two Englishmen put to death in Bukhara in 1842. He had them thrown from the top of a minaret for having ventured too far into Afghanistan. Such incidents made later travelers, like the French explorer J. P. Ferrier, fear for their own safety while in Afghanistan.

or the Russians. Instead, he played one power off against the other, and kept them both guessing as to where his real loyalties lay. He granted concessions to each, sought "advice" from each, and accepted handsome gifts—in the form of loans, railroads, and telegraph lines—from each. Neither the British nor the Russians could ever be sure of Nasiru'd Din, and so both were forced to maintain their vigilance at the Persian court, constantly striving to prevent one another from gaining the upper hand.

This war of nerves in Teheran was just one aspect of the increasing rivalry between Britain and Russia for supremacy in southwest Asia. With grim humor, a daring British Officer, Arthur Conolly, dubbed this contest the "Great Game." This ceased being merely a "game" during the Crimean War of 1854–6, but afterwards again became a series of moves and countermoves in the strategic territories

Above: nomads with their flocks in Afghanistan, pursuing a way of life that has remained the same for hundreds of years. The mountainous area was sparsely populated then as now, and the towns were small and primitive.

Above: J. P. Ferrier, who had been sent originally by the French to help organize the Persian army. After leaving Persia he went to Afghanistan, where he was promptly placed under surveillance by a local ruler, Yar Mohamed, who was convinced he was English. The Afghans were then still very bitter about the British attack on their land.

separating their two spheres of influence.

Late in the 1700's, the British had begun exploring Afghanistan. They justified their activities there as an extension of their geographical survey of northern India. But their real reason for exploring the country was political. The security of India depended on their knowing the sort of people and terrain that lay beyond it.

Two of the early British explorers in Afghanistan were named Christie and Pottinger. Disguised as horse-dealers, they crossed the country from east to west in 1810, and returned to India with the first rough sketch of the route to Herat, Afghanistan's largest city. Over the next 25 years, a number of other British survey teams made their way through the country, penetrating deep into the Hindu Kush mountains that link Afghanistan to Kashmir.

These expeditions paved the way for a successful British military campaign against Afghanistan in 1839. The campaign was launched in response to rumors that the Afghan ruler, Dost Mohamed, was considering an alliance with Russia. The very idea was enough to send shivers up British spines, and the East India Company promptly sent an armed force to change Dost Mohamed's mind. So powerful was the British advance that the Afghans offered little resistance. The British marched into the capital, Kabul, unopposed, and placed a puppet ruler on the Afghan throne.

The Afghans were extremely bitter about this act of aggression, as a French explorer named J. P. Ferrier discovered some years later. In 1845, he set out from Baghdad with the idea of reaching India by way of Afghanistan. He arrived at Herat from Persia and there was immediately put under surveillance by the local ruler, Yar Mohamed, who believed him to be an Englishman. For many days, Ferrier lived in fear of his life. He witnessed the hideous execution of a prisoner who had tried to escape. The man was blown from a gun: "A horrid spectacle. . . . The broken limbs . . . scattered in all directions [and] were in an instant devoured by the dogs that were loitering about the spot."

Fortunately, Ferrier himself was spared. Somehow he managed to convince Yar Mohamed that he was not British after all, and was granted leave to depart. He set off once more, making his way through a sweltering desert where the temperature in the sun was close to 150°F. Five years earlier a British traveler had poached eggs on the sizzling sand.

As Ferrier traveled east, he was constantly harassed by bandits and hostile tribesmen, and even pillaged by his own guides. In fact, the only reason he was not actually killed was that the Afghans were Moslems, and according to the Moslem code of hospitality, even an uninvited guest is sacred. A tribal chieftain who coveted Ferrier's pistols sighed, "You are my guest . . . may your shadow never be less! But it would have been a fine piece of good luck to meet you [far] from this place. Those pistols, that gun . . . would soon have been hung up in my house!"

Right: the Russian Prince Soltykoff on a visit to Persia, painting a young Persian prince. The Russians and the British vied with each other for years to gain influence over the Persian shah, Nasiru'd Din, who managed to extract the maximum benefit without committing himself to either side.

But not all Afghans adhered to the rules of hospitality. When Ferrier reached the little principality of Mahmoodabad, he was thrown into jail and robbed of his pistols. For three weeks he was kept in a vermin-infested hut and abused by his guards. Before being released, he was forced to part with all his money.

Ferrier pressed on to the city of Kandahar, in southern Afghanistan. There he was once again placed under house arrest. Unfortunately, his arrival in the city coincided with the outbreak of a cholera epidemic. The populace, believing that Allah had sent the

Above: Sir Percy Sykes, the Englishman who spent many years in Persia making six major expeditions to fill in large blank spaces on the map. During all his time there he remained enthusiastic about the quality of life in Persia.

epidemic because their ruler was harboring an unbeliever, rose up in arms and stormed the palace. Ferrier, who had had years of experience in the French army, persuaded the ruler to let him take charge of the palace troops, and under his expert guidance, they repelled the attack.

But even this act of heroism did not prevent Ferrier from ultimately being sent back to Herat as a "trouble-maker." Disgusted, Ferrier left Afghanistan, concluding that the only way to deal with the Afghans was "by force or by the hope of gain."

Force was the method used by the Russians in dealing with the Moslem people who dwelt in the vast region of steppes and deserts east of the Caspian Sea and south of Siberia. These people, like the Afghans, were nomadic tribesmen. They were no match for the

fierce Cossack armies that began sweeping down on them in the mid-1800's.

Russian expansion in this region was both systematic and relentless. It began in the 1840's, when teams of explorers were sent out to make a careful survey of the area between the northern shores of the Caspian Sea, the Aral Sea, and Lake Balkhash. From there, they worked their way south to the Syr-Darya River, and thence on down to the cluster of cities just north of Afghanistan. Inexorably, the work of the scientist was followed up by the work of the soldier, as the armies of the czar moved south to secure the newly explored territories. The city of Tashkent fell to the Russians in 1865, and the city of Bukhara in 1868. Samarkand, Khiva, and Kokand followed in quick succession. By 1880, only the region now called Turkmen-

Above: the Persian ambassador, Mirza Abul Hassan, making a splendid entrance into St. Petersburg in the early 1800's, during the period when Britain and Russia were struggling for influence over the shah. He had also represented the shah in London.

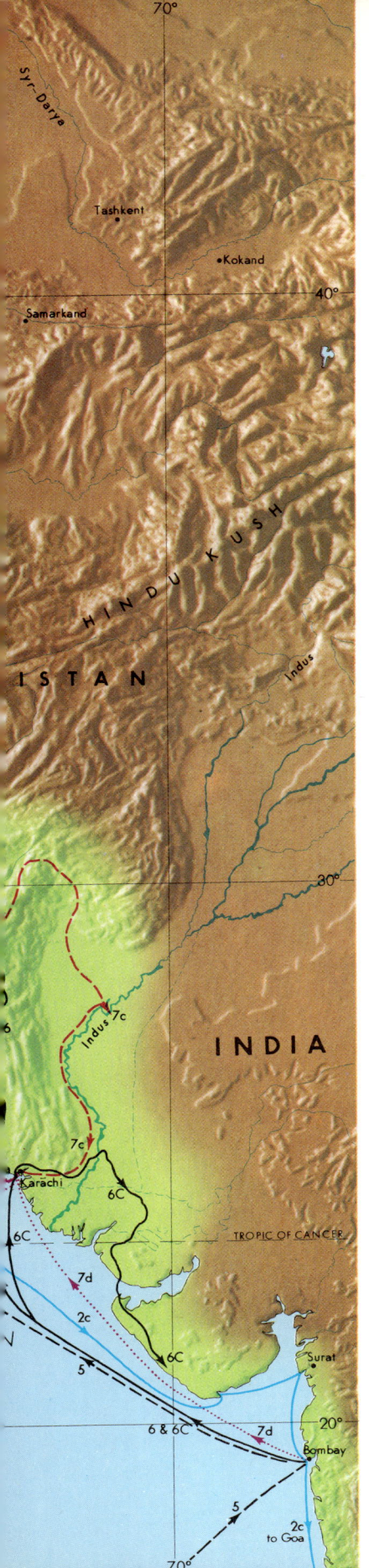

istan—between the Aral Sea and northern Persia—remained unconquered. And by 1884, that region, too, was in Russia's pocket.

These developments caused grave concern in British India. Suddenly, alarmingly, Russia was at the very gates of Kashmir, Afghanistan, *and* Persia. The British stepped up their own explorations west of India, and waged a new war against Afghanistan. By 1880, they were as much the masters of that country as the Russians were of the lands beyond it. This gave the British some measure of security, but they could not rest until they had mapped every corner of accessible ground between India and northwest Persia.

This new phase of British exploration began in 1864, with the expedition of a man named Sir Frederick Goldsmid. He and his men crisscrossed Persia and Afghanistan, as well as Baluchistan (a smaller kingdom along the shores of the Arabian Sea), which today forms a part of Pakistan. During the next 45 years, scores of other British explorers made their way through the three kingdoms, and, slowly but surely, the blank spaces on the map were filled in.

Among all the explorers of this difficult terrain, none ranks higher than Sir Percy Sykes. Between 1893 and 1910, he made no fewer than six major expeditions through Persia and Baluchistan. Each contributed significantly to British knowledge of the region, and each confirmed and increased Sykes's own love of Persia. His writings about the kingdom are full of glowing accounts of its romantic beauty. About one particularly lovely Persian garden, luxuriant with flowers and fruit trees, fountains and pavilions, he wrote that, "the singing of the nightingales, added to the murmur of the water and the scent of the roses, made us travelers . . . feel that we had reached an earthly Paradise."

But Sykes's romantic view of Persia was not shared by the majority of British travelers in the late 1800's. What they saw was a backward country "even more incapable than Turkey of adopting European habits," as one diplomat put it. Persia was in fact badly in need of modernization and reform. But neither the British nor the Russians were prepared to devote their time to improving conditions in the kingdom. They were too busy vying with each other for influence over the shah. On his side, Shah Nasiru'd Din graciously accepted the vast loans they offered him, and even went so far as to pay a series of state visits to London and St. Petersburg. But to the

The arrival of Shah Nasiru'd Din at Windsor Castle in 1873. Queen Victoria, standing on the steps, is greeting the shah. The Prince of Wales is with her, in the ceremonial uniform of a general of the British army.

exasperation of both sides, he still refused to commit himself one way or the other.

And then, in 1896, Nasiru'd Din was assassinated. A wave of agitation for governmental reform swept through the country and, in 1906, Nasiru'd Din's successor, Muzaffar u-Din, was forced to grant his people a constitution. Some Persian reformers were wary of expanding British and Russian influences in their country, which was still too weak to stand up to them. In 1907, in a high-handed agreement called the Anglo-Russian Convention, the two powers

settled their rivalry by dividing Persia into spheres of influence. There was a Russian zone in the north, containing most of Persia's main cities; a neutral zone in the center; and a British zone in the south, including many of the country's new oil fields.

The Anglo-Russian Convention became inoperative during World War I and was formally abandoned by the Soviet government in 1918. Nonetheless, the kingdom's strategic location and vast reserves of oil continued to make it a target of Soviet and Western imperialism until long after World War II.

In Oſtaſien

Confrontation in the Heartland

8

Nowhere did Russia and Britain play the "Great Game" of the 1800's as fiercely as they did in Central Asia and Tibet. There, knowledge was power—the power to protect and consolidate their rival empires. And, as the two nations jockeyed for position in this strategic corner of Asia, the work of their explorers took on a deadly political significance.

The Russians took a giant step toward Tibet in 1856, when an adventurous scientist named Semenov explored the Tien Shan mountains bordering Chinese Turkestan. His expedition fired the imagination of other Russian explorers, and over the next 50 years, they made a full-scale assault on the deserts and mountains south of Siberia. Some of these hardy pioneers mapped the rough Mongolian plateau and the southern reaches of the Altai mountain range. Others explored the Tien Shan and the bleak Taklamakan Desert.

The British were understandably alarmed by these maneuvers. Ostensibly, the Russians were exploring Central Asia in the pure interests of science. But the British knew only too well that earlier Russian exploration—in the region east of the Caspian—had heralded a series of conquests. Now Russian scientists were reconnoitering the region north of Tibet, and it was only too clear that the czar had his eye on the very mountain kingdom Britain needed to defend her Indian empire. This was a shattering prospect for the British. If Russia gained dominion over Tibet, there would be no stopping her—sooner or later, she would make a bid for India itself.

To a large degree, British fears were justified. For the previous 300 years, the Russian Empire had been growing at the phenomenal rate of 55 square miles a day. And if anything, Russian imperial ambitions had only grown stronger over the years. As India's British viceroy, Lord Curzon, put it, "Each morsel but whets her appetite for more, and inflames the passion for pan-Asiatic domination." Indeed, by the late 1800's, Russia had begun to regard the whole continent as her natural sphere of influence. And Tibet— strategically placed between China and India—was high on the czar's list of Asian priorities. Curzon guessed rightly when he surmised that the czar was encouraging Russian explorers to aim for Lhasa.

But access to the Tibetan capital proved just as problematical for the Russians as it was for Montgomerie's pundits. The forbidding rim of mountains along Tibet's northern plateau, combined with

Above: Nicholas I, czar of Russia. He commissioned Alexander von Humboldt to carry out scientific explorations in Siberia. It was during Nicholas' reign that Russia became involved in the "Great Game" with Great Britain.

Far left: a cartoon from a German political magazine showing an enormous Russian shoving a thin aristocratic Englishman along the bench of Central Asia, asking, "Do you mind moving?"

Left: Przhevalski was the giant of Russian exploration in Central Asia. Among other firsts, he was the first modern traveler to delineate the Altyn Tagh mountains that form a barrier to northern Tibet, and the first man to make a systematic survey of the sources of the Hwang Ho.

the Tibetan's morbid fear of foreigners, made the kingdom practically inaccessible. By 1900, only one Russian scientist had even succeeded in getting close to the sacred citadel. That man was Nikolai Przhevalski. Between 1870 and 1885, this tireless geographer made four attempts to reach Tibet, and, in the process, added more to the knowledge of Central Asia than any man before him.

With a small Cossack guard, Przhevalski began his first journey in northeastern Mongolia. From there he traveled to Peking, and then set out across the Ordos Desert, roughly following the route taken by Huc and Gabet 35 years before. Travel through this desert was never easy, especially for men making maps. "In the daytime," wrote Przhevalski, "the heat enveloped us on all sides, above from the sun, below from the burning ground. . . . To avoid the heat as much as possible, we rose before daybreak; tea-drinking and loading the camels, however, took up so much time that we never got away before four or even five o'clock in the morning. We might have lightened the fatigue considerably by night-marching, but in that case we would have had to forego the survey which formed so important a part of our labors."

At last, in October, 1872, the party reached the sparkling waters of the Koko Nor, just south of the Nan Shan mountains. But winter was setting in, and the pitiful state of his camels forced Przhevalski to turn back halfway across the vast Tibetan plateau. Ironically, he met precisely the same difficulties four years later, when he tried to penetrate Tibet from the direction of the Altyn Tagh mountains,

Below: Przhevalski's Cossack guard, an engraving from his book about his explorations. The Cossacks were loaned to him by the czar for the expedition, as part of the discreet backing the czar gave to Przhevalski's travels.

which lie west of the Nan Shan and south of the Taklamakan Desert.

In 1879, Przhevalski made his third—and most successful—journey to Tibet. This time he breached the mountain barrier, and began marching steadily southward through the plateau. But the Chinese ambassadors in Lhasa, learning of his approach, spread a rumor that the Russian was on his way to kidnap the Dalai Lama. Outraged, the Tibetans organized a small militia and began harassing the travelers. Finally, at a village just 170 miles from Lhasa, the explorer was met by a deputation of Tibetan officials, who absolutely forbade him to go a step farther. Practically within sight of his goal, the disappointed Russian was once more forced to turn back.

In 1883, the indefatigable geographer mustered a new party of 20 men for what was to be his last expedition in Tibet. Though yet again turned back in northern Tibet, he returned to Russia with much information about the northern reaches of the kingdom.

All the time Przhevalski was trying to reach Lhasa from the north, the British were trying to reach it from the south. But so far, only the pundits had succeeded. And meanwhile, the Russians were

Above: an engraving from Przhevalski's book showing the heartbreaking climax of his expedition of 1879–80, when a force of Tibetan guards attacked his camp and forced him to turn back before he reached Lhasa.

Above: Sir Francis Younghusband, the young British explorer who crossed Central Asia. He came of a conventional colonial background—his father and four of his uncles were in the Indian Army—and he went to India to serve as an officer in the cavalry in 1882.

Above right: Younghusband (on the left) with his two companions on the journey across the barren Gobi Desert.

making steady progress in Central Asia. Not to be outdone, the British, too, began exploring the heartland. Between 1873 and 1900, a number of expeditions traveled south from Siberia and west from China into the Taklamakan and Gobi deserts. But none of them made as long—or as daring—a journey into the heartland as a youthful British officer named Francis Younghusband.

Younghusband was a born adventurer. In 1886, at the age of 23, he accompanied a British expedition from Peking to Manchuria, and the very next year, set off on an epic journey across Central Asia. His plan was to reconnoitre the territory between Peking and Hami, at the western end of the Tien Shan, before proceeding to India. It was an enormous undertaking for someone who had never even been in a desert before. But Younghusband was a daredevil, and actually relished the prospect of danger and hardship.

Two weeks out of Peking, Younghusband and his two companions, a cook and an interpreter, reached the edge of the Gobi Desert. Here, at a small waystation, the young explorer obtained five camels and a guide to take his party westward. But before they could set out, they had to consult the Chinese calendar to fix the correct moment for their departure. "The guide was very particular about this," wrote Younghusband later, "He said it would never do to start in a casual way on a journey like this."

Finally, on April 26, 1887, the auspicious moment arrived, and the party set out for the desert oven. To enable the camels to feed during

NO THOROUGHFARE

TO LH'ASSA

FORCED FAVOURS.

The Grand Lama of Thibet. "NOW THEN, WHAT'S YOUR BUSINESS?"
British Lion. "I'VE COME TO BRING YOU THE BLESSINGS OF FREE TRADE."
The Grand L. "I'M A PROTECTIONIST. DON'T WANT 'EM."
British Lion. "WELL, YOU'VE *GOT TO HAVE* 'EM!"
["The advisers of the Dalai Lama, having ignored their obligations to us under the Convention of 1890, have now ignored the British Mission;"... "an advance is to be made into the Chumbi Valley on the frontier of Thibet."—*Daily Paper.*]

Above: a cartoon from the English satirical magazine *Punch,* ridiculing the British determination to open Tibet to the glories of British trade.

the day, the party traveled between 3 p.m. and midnight. Even at night the air was dry as a bone, and the men's belongings became charged with static electricity so that "in opening a sheepskin coat or blanket, a loud crackling noise would be given out, accompanied by a sheet of fire."

Toward the end of June, the tiny caravan reached the eastern end of the Nomin Gobi, a tongue of desert between the Altai and Tien Shan mountains. Crossing this desert was to prove the worst part of their journey. In his journal, Younghusband recorded that, "Nothing we have passed hitherto can compare with it—a succession of gravel ranges without any sign of life, animal or vegetable, and not a drop of water. . . ." But at long last, they reached the shade of the Karlik Tagh mountains, and dragged themselves into the town of Hami. Younghusband and his exhausted companions rested there for a few days, then set off once more. It took them less than two months to reach Kashgar, 1,000 miles southwest of Hami. But even at Kashgar, Younghusband's journey was not over. Proceeding south, he crossed the mighty Karakoram mountains— becoming the first European to ascend the lofty Mustagh Pass in Kashmir—and, in the fall of 1887, rejoined his regiment in India.

Over the next 10 years, Younghusband was to make a number of other exploratory journeys, mostly in the complex of ranges north- west of India. But his real ambition—like that of so many other British officers in India—was to explore Tibet. His chance to do so finally came in 1903, when he was chosen to head a crucial diplomatic mission to Lhasa.

By 1903, British anxiety about Russian activities in Tibet had reached fever pitch. Word had begun filtering through diplomatic channels that the czar now had a secret agent in the very palace of the Dalai Lama. The name of this sinister character was Arguan Dorjiev. Born a Buriat-Mongol in southeastern Siberia, he possessed Russian citizenship but he had resided in Tibet for 26 years. In his youth, Dorjiev had been trained as a Buddhist monk, so he had no trouble gaining access to Lhasa. Once there, he had insinuated himself among the lamas, risen rapidly in the ranks, and won the coveted job of tutor to the young Dalai Lama.

According to a Japanese observer then in the capital, the crafty Dorjiev had "omitted no pains to win the heart of his little pupil," and early on had begun advising him to make friends with Russia. Dorjiev told the boy that the czar was a Buddhist too, and would defend Tibet against the British. Dorjiev was so convincing that the Dalai Lama sent him on several visits to the Russian court in

Right: George Nathaniel Curzon, then viceroy of India and the instigator of Younghusband's expedition into Tibet. Lord Curzon was determined to provide a frontier-in-depth for India, a safe buffer area beyond the actual border.

Below: one of the Tibetan wounded at Guru. The battle—which was the result of a minor incident—quickly turned into a massacre, as the Tibetans were mowed down by British-led forces.

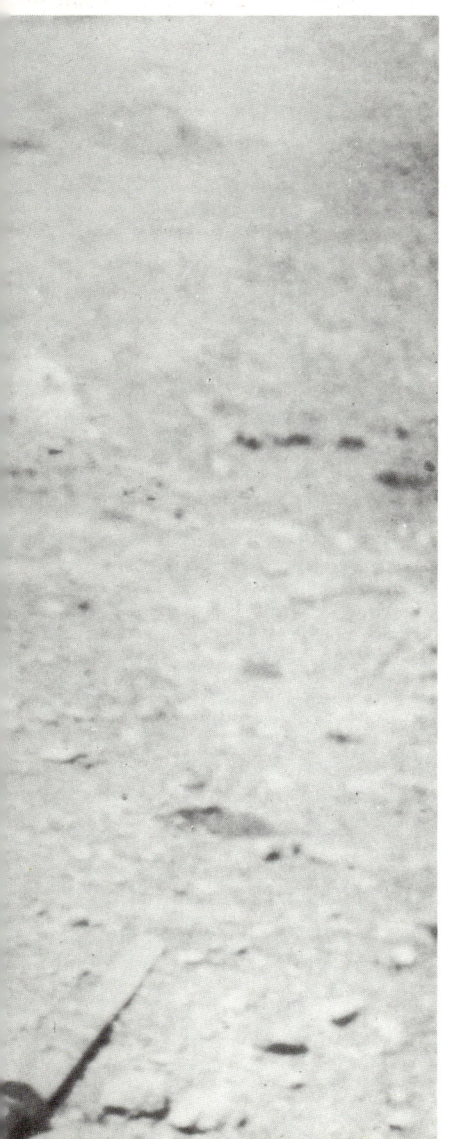

1898 to 1901. Dorjiev's welcome from the Russian royal family gave rise to alarming rumors of Russian influence in Tibet.

In 1903, Lord Curzon, viceroy of India, decided to counter Russian influence in Tibet with direct British pressure. He would send a mission to Lhasa and force the Dalai Lama to renounce his Russian affiliations. In Curzon's view, it was the only way to guarantee the safety of British India. Younghusband, picked to head the mission, gladly seized this opportunity to play the Great Game. "Here indeed, I felt, was the chance of my life. I was once more alive," he wrote.

The expedition that set out for Lhasa in 1903 was almost an invasionary force. Younghusband had a military "escort" of 1,150 Indian soldiers under the command of a British general named Macdonald. In addition, there were 10,000 Indian tribesmen to carry baggage, and no fewer than 20,000 animals. Included in this traveling

Below: a pencil drawing by N. Rybot of Lieutenant Hadow at Gyantse, on the mission roof. Hadow had also been at Guru, of which he wrote, "I hope I shall never have to shoot down men *walking* away again," as the Tibetans retreated.

zoo were mules, yaks, camels, buffalo, bullocks, horses, pack ponies, and even two "zebrules"—experimental animals half mule and half zebra. Sadly, many of the animals perished in the long climb from the hot forests of northern India to the icy passes of the Himalaya.

When Younghusband reached southern Tibet, he was greeted by a party of Tibetan officials who told him that any Anglo-Tibetan negotiations could be held only on the India-Tibet frontier. Never, never, they said, would Europeans be allowed inside their sacred city (Lhasa). But the British kept advancing, and by January, 1904, were on the Guru plain, 150 miles southwest of the city. There they were met by an armed force of 2,000 Tibetan warriors.

There was a curious period of indecision as the two armies faced each other; neither side seemed willing to open fire. Then the British began trying to shoulder their way through the Tibetan ranks like policemen handling an unruly crowd. This was too much for the Tibetan general; he pulled out his revolver and shot one of the Indian soldiers. At once the British attacked and, with a thundering volley of rifle shots, mowed down the Tibetan soldiers.

This crushing defeat was repeated 50 miles farther north on July 6, 1904, when the infantry led a full-scale attack on the Tibetan *dzong* (fort) outside the town of Gyantse. Although vastly outnumbered, the British soon gained the upper hand. Younghusband

Above: a drawing in crayon by N. Rybot of the Tsechen lamasery near Gyantse, which the British took. Rybot noted on the drawing, "Captured 28 June 04 Looted 29 June 04 Burnt 5 July 04."

reports that, "Tier after tier of the fortification was crowned, and at last our men were seen placing the Union Jack on the highest pinnacle of the Dzong. The Tibetans had fled precipitously, and Gyantse was ours."

Triumphant, the British marched into Lhasa on August 3, 1904. They were the first Europeans to see the forbidden city since Huc and Gabet, over 50 years before. It was a glorious moment for Younghusband: "The goal of so many travelers' ambitions was actually in sight. . . . The sacred city, hidden so far and deep behind the Himalayan ramparts, and so jealously guarded from strangers, was full before our eyes."

Both the Dalai Lama and the treacherous Dorjiev had fled the capital by the time Younghusband arrived. The Tibetan regent, left to deal with the conquerors, was prepared to enter into negotiations with the British as the Russians showed no inclination to come to the Dalai Lama's aid. Now the regent had no choice but to grant the sweeping demands Younghusband made on behalf of Britain.

But ironically, as Younghusband learned when he returned to India, he had gained *too much* for Britain. Upon publication of Younghusband's proposed treaty between Britain and Tibet, serious

Left: a photograph of the 13th Dalai Lama (1876–1933) when he was 24. He fled with his tutor, the Mongol Dorjiev, as Younghusband's British forces neared the Tibetan capital.

Below: Central Asia. In this forbidding terrain of burning sands and rocky wastes, jagged peaks and windswept plateaus, Nikolai Przhevalski, Francis Younghusband, and Sven Hedin carried out extensive explorations, pioneering routes through territories never before seen by any European.

Przhevalski

1a	1870–3
1b	1876–7
1c	1879–80
1d	1883–5
1e	1888

Younghusband

2b	1886
2c	1887
2d	1889
2e	1890–1
2f	1892–5

Younghusband (with Macdonald) 2g 1903–4

Hedin	3a	1890–1
Hedin	3b	1893–7
Hedin	3c	1899–1902
Hedin	3d	1906–8
Hedin Sino-Swedish expedition	3e	1927–33
Other members of the Sino-Swedish expedition	3E	
Hedin Sino-Swedish expedition	3f	1933–5

© Geographical Projects   114°

Top: a watercolor drawing by Sven Hedin of one of his mountain camps. The drawing, dated 1908, was made during his second journey to Tibet.

Above: Sven Hedin sitting on a camel outside a yurt in Mongolia, on his way to Peking. Hedin managed to learn the rudiments of the Mongolian language by persuading a Mongol yak-hunter to act as his tutor, miming the words that he wanted to learn.

protests were raised by the governments of Germany, Russia and China. It was claimed that British dominion over the mountain country would upset the delicate balance of power in Asia. There was only one answer: Younghusband's agreement with Tibet had to be modified. In 1906, Britain made a treaty with Peking recognizing China's suzerainty over Tibet. This arrangement also suited the czar, and in 1907 Russia and Britain signed a treaty formally recognizing this diplomatic solution to the "problem" of Tibet.

The Great Game in Central Asia was now officially over. But exploration in the heartland continued, and, if anything, became more ambitious and more spectacular in the early decades of the 1900's. The two leading figures in this period of exploration were Sven Hedin and Sir Aurel Stein. The two men were as different from one another as night and day, but each was to make discoveries in Central Asia that astonished the world.

Sven Hedin was a bit like Francis Younghusband. Rugged, fearless, and supremely self-confident, he had an unquenchable thirst for adventure. In 1890, as a 25-year-old member of the Swedish embassy in Persia, he made a trip eastward to Kashgar, and crossed the Tien Shan mountains. This taste of Asian travel merely whetted his appetite for more, and in 1893, he was off again, seeking "the road to wild adventure" in the Taklamakan Desert. But young Hedin was still a relatively inexperienced desert traveler, and he almost perished during his first few weeks in the desert.

Some 200 miles out of Kashgar, his caravan began to run short of water. Hedin was prepared to turn back, but his guides, believing that the Khotan River was not far off, persuaded him to press on. He strictly rationed their remaining water, but even so, the last of their meagre supply was soon gone. A week went by, and still they saw no sign of the river. They were lost! One by one, the expedition's animals began to die. The men themselves were so desperate for liquid that they killed a sheep and tried to drink its blood. But the fluid was so thick that none of them could swallow it. During the next few gruesome days, death struck down man after man. At last, only Hedin and his faithful servant Kasim had strength enough to continue the struggle.

The two survivors dragged themselves forward over the dunes, toiling on "for life—bare life," writes Hedin. At last, like a miracle, a dark green line showed itself on the horizon. It was the poplar wood along the banks of the Khotan River. But Kasim could go no farther. He fell down in the sand, his eyes vacant, waiting for death. Alone, Hedin staggered forward to the promise of water. But when he reached the Khotan, he found the river bed dry! Somehow, this awful discovery only made the young Swede more determined than ever not to die—especially not in the very bed of a river. Grimly, he plodded on, as if "led by an unseen, but irresistible hand." Then, suddenly, he heard a splash, and saw a wild duck fly up into the air. A few paces farther on, he found a clear pool in the deepest part of the river bed. "I drank, and drank, and drank," he wrote later. Then, having filled his boots with water, he returned to revive Kasim. Soon afterward, the two were rescued by some passing shepherds.

Hedin returned to Kashgar, and, after a short expedition to the Pamirs, again set out for the desert. By now he was more familiar with the perils of the Taklamakan, but it still held some grim challenges. One of these was the *kara-buran* (black desert-storm). When a kara-buran hit the caravan, there was nothing to do but

Above: two Tibetan youths exchanging a traditional form of greeting. These illustrations and those overleaf are taken from a portfolio of many hundreds of drawings and watercolors made by Sven Hedin during his travels.

Below: a Tibetan woman wearing traditional multicolored woolen garments.

wrap up and lay low while the wind screamed around the tents and the sky grew dark with flying sand. On a later expedition, Hedin reports that one of these storms "lasted all day, all night, and part of the next day, and when at last it had shot past . . . we felt queerly dazed, as after a long illness."

Before entering the Taklamakan, Hedin had heard rumors of enchanted ruins to be found in the forbidding desert. He therefore hired guides who claimed to know their location. Within days of entering the desert, he was led to a forest of ancient timber posts. He and his men started digging and discovered amazing relics of a 2,000-year-old city. Hedin carefully marked the site before proceeding eastward. The explorer later found another ancient city buried in the sands of the Taklamakan, and these discoveries brought him world fame on his return to Europe in 1897.

But Hedin was essentially an explorer, not an archaeologist, and he was content to leave the scientific examination of his cities to other men. He now wanted to explore Tibet, and on his third expedition, in 1899, made a heroic attempt to reach Lhasa from Kashgar. But a mere 150 miles from the forbidden city, he was turned back, as Przhevalski had been, by a party of Tibetan officials. "It is quite beyond any need," they declared quaintly, "for Europeans to enter the Land of the Holy Books." Hedin was forced to turn west, making

Above: a lama at the door of a Tibetan mausoleum. Like Przhevalski, Hedin was forced to turn away before he reached the forbidden city of Lhasa, and had to go to India by way of Leh.

Left: a Tibetan soldier, armed with an old-fashioned type of musket. It was this sort of weapon that the Tibetans tried to use to repulse the British.

Right: a beggar pleading for alms.

his way over the mountains to India via the Ladakh city of Leh.

It was from Leh that Hedin started on his fourth and greatest expedition in 1906. His object this time was to explore the valley of the Tsangpo River (sometimes also called the Upper Brahmaputra) which flows through southern Tibet. But first he had to cross the Himalaya, and winter overtook his party as they struggled over the high passes. Most of his pack horses died in the heights, and only a hastily improvised felt jacket saved the life of one of his dogs.

But at last Hedin reached the beautiful valley of the Tsangpo and began following the river eastward, past fields of ferns and snow-capped mountains, toward the town of Shigatse—last visited by Samuel Turner of the English East India Company in 1783. Hedin was granted permission to enter the nearby lamasery of Tashilhumpo. Several monks conducted him through long narrow lanes to the sacred

Above: a photograph taken by Sir Aurel Stein during his excavations near Khotan. The local workmen he employed are shown in the emerging ruins. Stein was first attracted to the desert by reading Hedin's report of ancient cities still lying beneath dry desert sands.

library, a vast hall filled with Buddhist holy books, and showed him the cavernous kitchen where tea was brewed for the building's 3,800 lamas. But the most amazing thing Hedin saw was 100 miles beyond the lamasery. This was a *dupkang*, or hermit dwelling. The entrance was sealed up, leaving only a small hole through which the man inside received his daily ration of food. Hedin was told that voluntary imprisonment of this kind earned a man *nirvana* (the "blessed oblivion") after death. One poor soul who had been locked up for 69 years asked to be let out just before he died, to see the sun once more. But when the old hermit emerged, he was found to be stone-blind, and died almost immediately.

After leaving Shigatse, Hedin turned west again, and made two major discoveries. The first was the source of the Tsangpo River: a blue-green glacier high in the mountains of western Tibet. The second was the source of the Indus River: a little stream gushing from a shelf of rock just north of the sacred Lake Manasarowar in southwestern Tibet. These two discoveries—made within the space of a few months—placed Hedin among the ranks of Tibet's most distinguished explorers.

While the Swedish adventurer was cutting a swathe through the

Above: Aurel Stein (1862-1943). He was a quiet and unassuming man who took great pains to record all his discoveries carefully, taking many thousands of photographs and writing numerous books about his amazing finds.

deserts and mountains of the heartland, another remarkable explorer was also at work in Central Asia. This was Sir Aurel Stein. A shy, unassuming scholar, Stein was Hedin's complete opposite in every respect except one: he, too, was fascinated by the mysteries of the Asian interior. Born in Budapest, Stein had emigrated to England as a young man, and taken up Asian studies. He was particularly interested in the early history of the continent, and was enthralled in 1897 by Hedin's report of ancient cities beneath the sands of the desert corridor. In 1900–1901, Stein himself made a reconnaissance of the southern Taklamakan, and returned convinced that it held a wealth of archaeological treasures.

In 1906, Stein returned to the Taklamakan in charge of a large expedition. At a site just beyond Khotan, he found a collection of ancient wooden tablets still bearing their original clay seals. The seals depicted the gods Eros and Hercules—proof that once, long ago, the people of Central Asia had had tangible links with Greece and Rome. At a site discovered by Hedin in 1900 near the Lop Nor, Stein unearthed bales of yellow silk, bronze mirrors, rings, bells, and scraps of manuscript. These relics indicated that the site might have been a frontier town on the ancient Silk Road between China and

Rome. Where now there was desert, there had once been a bustling town, with many houses, several official residences, and a bricked-based shrine. Southwest of Loulan, at an ancient ruin called Miran, Stein found several giant statues, including a bust of Buddha, and a crumbling bit of manuscript that, when later deciphered, turned out to be a recipe for a medicine concocted of butter, barley, and boiled sheep's dung!

All these finds were excavated by Stein and his men under grueling desert conditions—the same intensely dry heat, in fact, that had preserved these buried cities for almost 2,000 years. Stein's work proved conclusively that hundreds of years ago, Central Asia contained large tracts of fertile land, watered by numerous rivers and inhabited by thriving populations. One of the ruins Stein explored was 100 miles from any drinkable water, an indication of how dramatically the climate and geography of the region had changed since ancient times.

Slowly, Stein worked his way from one site to another. Then, one day, as he was approaching the western end of the Gobi Desert, he spied a solid mass of brickwork, 23 feet high. Was it an ancient watchtower? After clearing away the sand at the base of the tower, the archaeologist found the remains of a regular wall made of reed bundles set in a mixture of clay and gravel. On sighting another watchtower 3 miles along the wall, Stein correctly concluded that the wall was part of an ancient Chinese fortification.

But Stein's greatest discovery still lay ahead. Following the reed wall, he came to a towering cliff-face just outside the Chinese outpost of Tunhwang. The cliff was honeycombed with small caves, linked together by crumbling flights of steps. All these so-called "Caves of the Thousand Buddhas" had once been shrines, and many were lavishly decorated with wall paintings. In Tunhwang, Stein learned that a hoard of manuscripts had recently been found in one of the caves. With some difficulty, he persuaded the keeper of the shrines to show him a few of these *chings*, or sacred texts. The man brought out a few specimens. All were of great antiquity, and in remarkably good condition. There were manuscripts, scroll paintings on fine Chinese silk, and packets of long, brilliantly colored temple banners.

What Stein held in his hands were the remnants of a long-forgotten library, a priceless record of China's past greatness. Excitedly, the scholar asked if he might remove some of the manuscripts for closer inspection. The priest was dubious, but Stein overcame his objections with a generous donation of silver "for the upkeep of the shrines." A bargain was struck, and Stein came away with 29 cases containing 9,000 manuscripts and countless works of art. Much of this treasure trove is now housed in London's British Museum.

Stein's return from Central Asia in 1908 coincided with Hedin's return from Tibet. The paths of the two men were to cross many times during the next 25 years, as both men continued their ex-

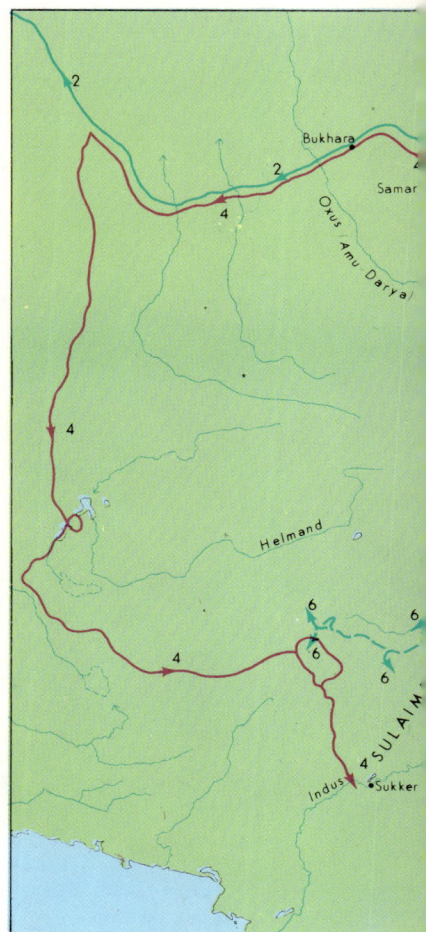

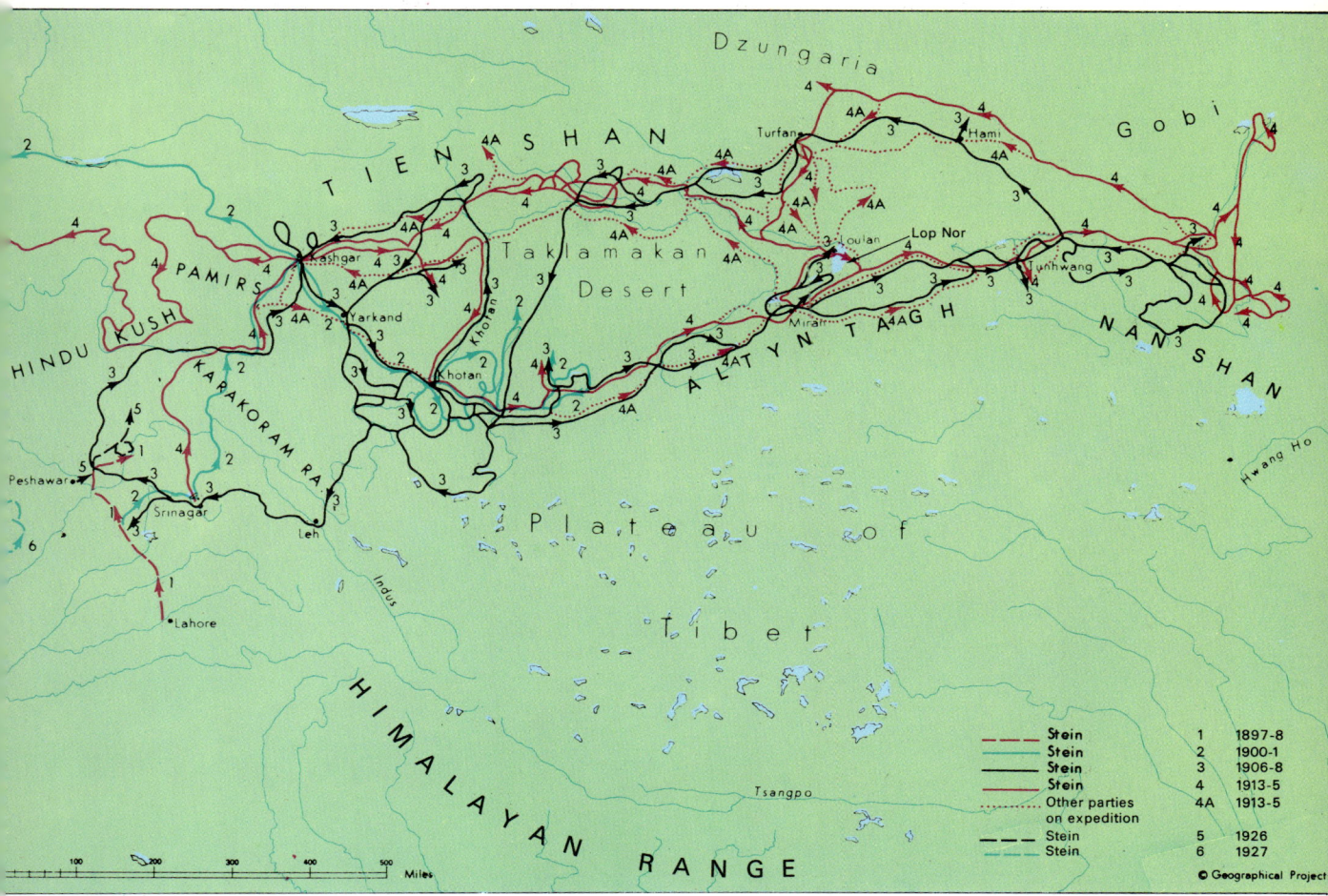

Above: the expeditions of Sir Aurel
Stein, 1897–1927. In the course of
his four major journeys, this remarkable
scientist ranged far and wide through
the Asian heartland, crisscrossing
the whole region between the
western borders of Afghanistan and
the Nan Shan mountains of China.

Left: a Chinese wooden votive tablet
that Stein found at Khotan. Like many
of his archaeological finds, it is now
kept in the British Museum in London.

plorations in the heartland. But Stein and Hedin were to be among
the last western European explorers in western China. After the
Chinese Communists came to power in 1949, access to much of the
heartland was again denied to travelers from the West.

In a curious way, history had repeated itself. It was like a flashback
to the Middle Ages—only instead of the hard-riding Mongols,
there were efficient Chinese border patrols to seal off the interior.
And as China strengthened its grip on Central Asia, only Russia,
secure in its Siberian holdings, could rival it for territorial supremacy
in Asia. Even remote Tibet was sucked into China's maw in the
1950's, when a Chinese army swept down on the kingdom and
wrested away its last shreds of independence. Only the countries
along Asia's southern perimeter remained free and open to Western
travelers.

But there are signs now that the long Red curtain may be lifted.
And when it is, explorers will once more find themselves drawn to
the hidden corners of the Asian wilderness. For, despite all the
stunning achievements of the Cossacks and merchants, missionaries
and scientists, few regions of the world still remain as mysterious
and challenging as the heartland of Asia.

Right: sunset in the desert—a time that most camel caravans welcome as a respite from the seemingly endless plodding through burning wastes of sand under a relentless sun. The drawing is by Sven Hedin.

Appendix

Left: Tibetan refugees from the Chinese now living in Switzerland. Many of the refugees are being trained for industrial work so that if it does become possible for them to return to Tibet, they will be more self-reliant.

If it were now possible for us to meet the men whose exploits are covered in this volume, we would probably find it hard to believe that they had all been pioneers. Indeed, only the most modern of them—men such as Younghusband, Przhevalski, Hedin, and Sykes—would really live up to our traditional image of the explorer. Yet every one of them, from the hardworking merchant-ambassadors and spirited Cossacks to the dedicated Jesuits, pundits, surveyors, and scientists, played a distinguished role in unraveling the mysteries of the Asian heartland. And, despite the wide differences in their backgrounds, motivations, and temperaments, each possessed the essential ingredients of the explorer: an unquenchable love of the unknown, and the kind of courage and determination that makes it possible for a man to achieve great things despite terrible hardships.

Nothing quite captures this spirit of adventure like the words of the men themselves. Throughout *The Heartland of Asia,* quotations from the explorers' own accounts of their travels have been included wherever possible. The first 20 pages of this Appendix offer the reader a chance to come one step closer to Asia's pioneers through longer excerpts from their writings. Here, in the words—and often, as well, the paintings and drawings—of such men as the scholarly priests Chappe d'Auteroche and Evarist Huc, the eloquent ambassadors James Morier and George Bogle, and the dauntless adventurers Sven Hedin and Francis Younghusband, the true drama of Asian exploration springs vividly to life.

Following this selection of firsthand narratives is a brief biographical dictionary of the main explorers covered in this book. In cases where the traveler's route has not already been mapped in the text, his biography is accompanied by a small route map.

After the biographical section there is a glossary of foreign and unfamiliar words and phrases used in the text. An index and a list of picture credits for *The Heartland of Asia* completes the Appendix.

Slaughter at Novgorod

Right: the Patriarch of the Russian Church and the czar in the great square in front of the Kremlin. In the background stands the church of St. Basil.

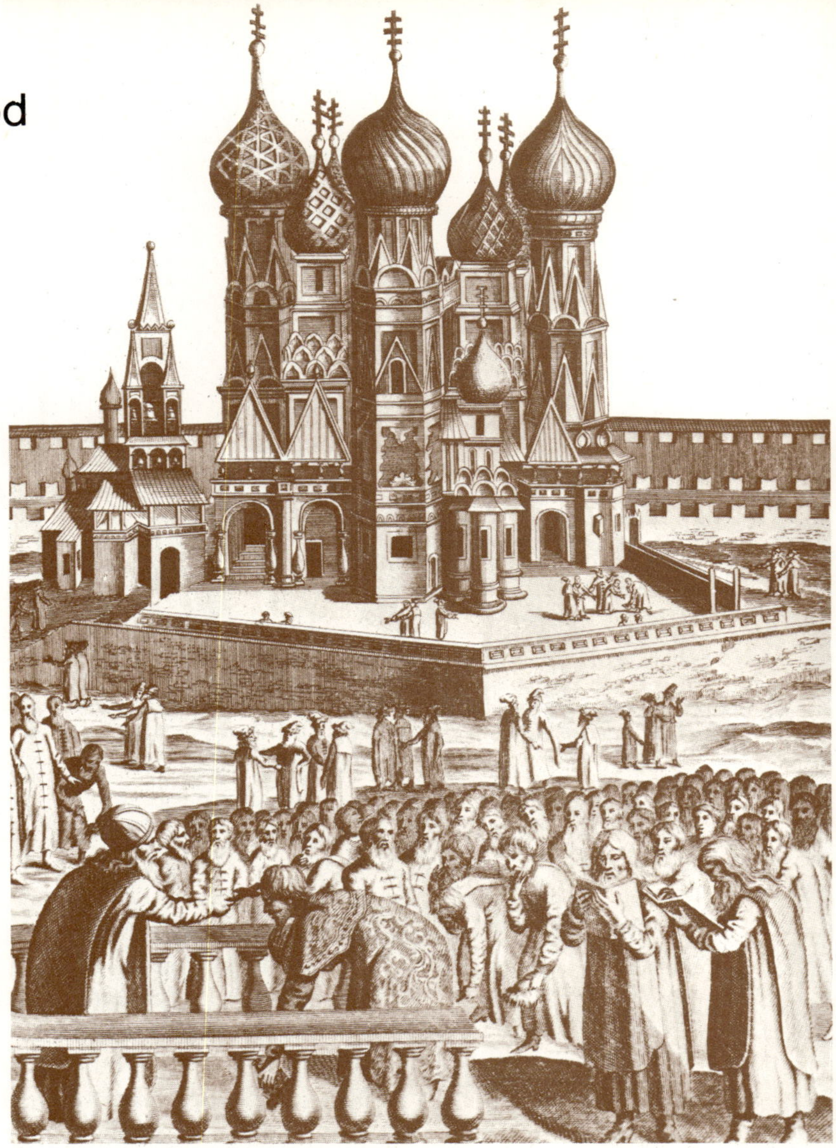

Ivan the Terrible had been dead for 50 years when Adam Olearius first arrived in Moscow with the Holstein embassy. But the dead czar was not forgotten; his legend lived on in countless stories about his insane cruelty. One such story, which Olearius recounts here, was told to him during his second visit to Russia in 1636.

"It is known that in 1569, because Ivan IV suspected (falsely) that his stepbrother . . . and the Novgorodians had hatched a plot against him and had appealed to the King of Poland for support, that ferocious monster [Ivan] fell upon Novgorod with an army. He and his soldiers slaughtered everyone they came upon in and around the city, hacked many people to pieces, drove a great crowd onto a long bridge and hurled them into the river, and caused a slaughter the like of which had never before been known in Russia. In this massacre 2,770 notable citizens perished, not counting women,

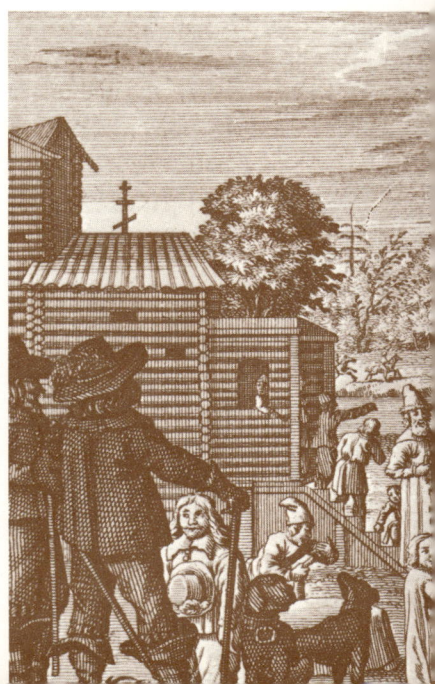

Above: an engraving from Olearius'
book, showing a Russian. He said that
the men dressed much like the Greeks.

Below: Olearius noted how important
religion was to the Russians. This
scene shows the Blessing of the Waters.

children, and the common people. . . . The Volkhov River was so filled with the corpses of the thousands so pitifully slain that its proper flow was impeded. It overflowed its banks and ran through the fields. . . .

"After the tyrannical Grand Prince [Ivan] had committed the above-mentioned inhuman massacre, the frightened archbishop who governed in the city invited him to dinner, in order to ingratiate himself. The tyrant did not refuse, and at the appointed hour he appeared with his armed bodyguards and suite. During the meal, he sent [his men] to sack the Church of St. Sophia, which was rich in gold and silver (the notables stored their valuables there, considering it a safe place). After dinner, he robbed the archbishop of all his costly vestments, episcopal ornaments, and finery, and said: 'You would do better as a bagpiper, leading a bear about and making him dance for money. You shall take a wife whom I have sought out and designated.' To the abbots and prioresses, who had fled from the monasteries into the city and were present at the dinner, he said: 'You all must appear at the archbishop's wedding. I hereby invite you, but you must bring good wedding presents.' He then ordered each of them to pay a certain sum, depending upon his estimate of their substance, and by threats forced them to comply.

"However, the czar took the money himself, ordered a white mare in foal for the archbishop, and pointing to it with his finger said: 'Look, here is your wife. Sit on her and ride to Moscow. There I will order that you be registered in the pipers' guild, so that you can play for a dancing bear.' The poor wretch was forced to mount the horse, in a coarse cloth robe, and his legs were tied under the horse's stomach; on his neck they hung a lyre, a zither, and pipes, and thus he had to ride through Novgorod, playing on the pipes. Since he had never learned to play, it may well be imagined how the music sounded. With this humiliation the tyrant let the archbishop escape. But the abbots and monks he executed in various horrible ways. . . .

"Then came the turn of one of the foremost wealthy citizens, Feodor Syrkov. He was brought to a camp not far from Novgorod . . . . Then he [Ivan] ordered that Feodor be set up to the knees in a cauldron full of boiling water and that his legs be cooked until he revealed where his gold and treasure was hidden (for he was a very rich man, who had built and maintained at his own expense 12 monasteries). After the tormented man ordered 30,000 silver guilders brought, the tyrant ordered him and his brother Aleksei to be hacked to pieces and cast into the river.

"Such were the horrible massacres inflicted on the people of Novgorod, and such was the fall of that good city, which saw how poorly it could stand against any power."

The Travels of Olearius in Seventeenth-Century Russia, *trans. and ed. by Samuel H. Baron (Stanford University Press: Stanford, California, 1967) pp. 90–92.*

By Sledge to Siberia

In the 1700's, travel by sledge (sleigh) through the snows of **Russia and Siberia could be a very hazardous undertaking, as the French scientist Chappe d'Auteroche makes vividly clear.**

"The surface of the Volga was as smooth as glass. . . . The snow which had fallen on it had been immediately carried off by the wind, and the sledges went on with inconceivable swiftness. I sometimes got out of my sledge and placed myself behind it in order to enjoy the pleasure of traveling so quick. The borders of the Volga are well

Left: a Samoyed woman and her child. The two are wearing fur clothing—the child's coat still has the head of the bear on the back.

Below: an engraving after a sketch by D'Auteroche of the teams of sledges in which he traveled from St. Petersburg.

peopled in the course of this route, so that the pleasure was heightened by seeing the river covered with a number of sledges crossing each other, running foul of, and frequently overturning each other . . . . The horses in common use are extremely small and appear weak, but they are inured to labor and get on very fast, although the postilions [drivers] seldom lash them. They content themselves with whistling to them and waving their hands, or speaking to them. They call these animals 'mother,' 'sister,' or 'dearly beloved'; one would imagine they are conversing with reasonable beings. . . .

"My journey after this was always toward the north. The cold and the snow increased daily, and houses were less frequently to be met with. . . . The roads were so narrow that there was but just room enough for a sledge, and moreover, so serpentine, that we were much incommoded by striking perpetually against the trees. The holes we likewise fell into every instant gave us such violent shocks that I was in continual fear lest the sledges should be broken to pieces. . . .

"My attendants did not relish this kind of life, and as they had no particular point in view to encourage them, they took some opportunity every day of showing their dissatisfaction. [Once,] I had no sooner got on a few [miles] into the wood, than I fell fast asleep. Sometime after I waked, it was still dark night, so that I could distinguish objects only from the clearness of the snow, much shaded by a cloudy sky. I knew not at first whether I was awake or in a dream, where I was or where I was going. But no sooner was I roused from this state of uncertainty than I was seized with the dreadful idea of being forsaken by my attendants.

"Getting immediately out of my sledge, I found myself alone. I called out to each person by his name, but all was silent around me. . . . The horror of my situation will easily be conceived when I found myself alone in one of the darkest nights . . . in the midst of the frosts and snows of Siberia. . . .

"Agitated with these thoughts, I replaced myself in the sledge, and got out of it again directly; the minute after, I got into it again . . . I went backward and forward in this manner a great part of the night, my thoughts always employed on my situation, and coming back now and then to my sledge. Although I was exposed to the most severe cold, I was still in a profuse sweat, notwithstanding I did not walk much. At last, pursuing the same track again, I perceived a glimmering light at some distance. On drawing near, I discovered it to be a house. I went in immediately, and found my people there asleep. . . . I roused my servant, however, and left the house as quick as I could, for I was unwilling they should discover how rejoiced I was at finding them again. A light was soon brought, and I found they had left the other sledges at the bottom of the village. . . . It was evident that I was obliged to put up with this affair!"

A Journey into Siberia, *Chappe d'Auteroche (London: 1770) pp. 38, 40, 46, 47.*

Upheaval in Astrabad

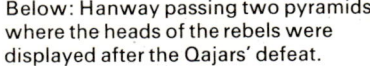

In the first of these two extracts from his writings, Jonas Hanway recounts how he was robbed by the Qajar rebels who stormed the Persian city of Astrabad shortly after his arrival in 1744. In the second passage, he describes how he returned to Astrabad several months later—after the city had been retaken by the shah's forces—and won compensation for his goods.

"The 15th of January, 1744, the dismal scene now began to disclose itself. . . . I heard the hoarse sound of trumpets; this was an alarm to call in the neighboring inhabitants, and to bring their cattle with them. The shops were ordered to be shut up, and the townsmen to repair to the walls to put them in a condition of defense. . . .

"I had ordered a watch to be kept all night, that I might not be surprised, and . . . slept till 4 in the morning. I was then awakened by a brisk but irregular discharge of musketry. A silence ensued, from whence I concluded the city was delivered up to Mahommed Hasen Beg [the leader of the rebels]. . . .

"It was now my turn to receive a visit from them and hear my fate. Sadoc Aga, who was appointed a general, with Mahommed Khan Beg—both young men of more fire than judgment—headed a party of 14 armed persons . . . and came to my house. I had collected my servants in one room, from whence I sent a little boy . . .

Left: the executions after the Qajar rebellion, when the authorities had reestablished control in Astrabad.

to conduct these hostile visitors to us, and to tell them that, as we were at their mercy, we hoped they would treat us with humanity. They immediately entered, and assured us they did not mean to hurt us; on the contrary, that as soon as their government was established, they would pay me for my goods. They demanded . . . where they were lodged, and informed me that the 40 bales [of cloth] which I had sent out of the town some days before were already in their possession. . . .

*   *   *   *

"The 16th of May we entered the city of Astrabad for the second time. . . . Upon my arrival, I was informed that the executions of that day consisted in cutting out the left eyes of thirty men, beheading four, and burning one alive, the last having been a captain in the rebel guard. . . . I sent a present to Behbud Khan, the king's general, and immediately followed it myself. He was . . . judging and condemning the unhappy rebels, who were brought to him one or two at a time, as he demanded them. After the compliments of welcome, he asked me why I did not stay in Astrabad till he came? As I knew nothing of him when I left the place, I thought the question a little extraordinary. I told him I did not remain in Astrabad because I was afraid of violence to my person . . . moreover, that it was my business to seek justice of the shah, whose decree I had now the honor to present him. . . .

"The king [had] ordered the money to be paid according to the account I should deliver. . . . The general . . . assured me it should be done without delay and spoke as follows: 'You find how the rebels have changed their blood for your crimson cloth. If it pleases the almighty to give the king health, no attempt of this sort will prevail against him.' He then presented me sweetmeats [cakes and candies] and large white mulberries, which are a delicious fruit; the prisoners were taken from his presence while we ate. In the interim, the secretary made a complimental speech on the general usefulness of merchants, observing 'that they brought wealth into countries, were serviceable to kings, and ought not to be offended by any, but protected by all parties.' "

An Historical Account of the British Trade Over the Caspian Sea, *Jonas Hanway (London: 1753) pp. 192, 196–197, 296–297.*

New Year in Tibet

In 1774, George Bogle—then only 28 years old—became the first British representative to visit Tibet. As these extracts from his journal illustrate, the young envoy was both touched and amused by the strange ways of the kingdom's gentle, good-humored people.

"The holidays of the new year drew nigh, and the [Panchen] Lama's relations came from different parts of the country to pay their respects to him. . . . I waited upon . . . the Chum Cusho [the Lama's sister-in-law], a cheerful widow of about five-and-forty, with a ruddy complexion and the remains of having once been handsome. In her younger days she was a nun, and her husband, the Lama's brother, a *gylong* [Buddhist monk]. But they happened somehow to form such a connection together as put an end to their state of celibacy. The Lama was much displeased with his brother, and would not admit him into his presence for many years. After his death, Chum Cusho, being past the heyday of life, resumed her religious character, and having taken up her vows of chastity, laid aside all her ornaments, dressed herself in homely garb, and set out on pilgrimages. . . . The Lama has since behaved to her and her children with much kindness. Her sons, the Pyn Cushos, and her daughters, the *annís* [Buddhist nuns] were present. . . .

"From the civilities which the Teshu [Panchen] Lama and everybody about him had shown me . . . I resolved to make some presents to the Lama's relations, and accordingly purchased coral beads, which are much valued in this part of the world. I carried them with me on my visit to the Chum Cusho and her daughters, and had much ado to procure their acceptance of them. The Pyn Cushos were still more difficult, and I believe I spent an hour in their tent before I could get them to agree to take my beads. 'You,' said they, 'are come from a far country. It is our business to render your stay agreeable. Why should you make us presents?'

"On the first day of the Tibetan year, everybody except the Lama assembled in the large court which is under the palace. All the galleries which ran round it were crowded with spectators. I was placed, as usual . . . in the highest balcony. The exhibitions began with dancing by merry Andrews [clowns] in masks. Then a number of banners were set up, and a crowd of gylongs dressed in various colored habits, with their cymbals and tabors [little drums] . . .

Above: a photograph taken in 1920 of a group of Tibetan nuns, some of whom are seen holding their prayer wheels.

Left: the home of the Tessaling Lama in Tibet, one of the distinctively Tibetan examples of architecture.

marched in procession round the court. . . . After this, the figure of a man, chalked upon paper, was laid upon the ground. Many strange ceremonies, which to me, who did not understand them, appeared whimsical, were performed about it, and a great fire being kindled in a corner of the court, it was at length held over it and . . . vanished with much smoke and explosion. I was told it was a figure of the devil, but am not sufficiently skilled in the Tibetan mythology to enter into particulars. One thing is certain, it was painted white, with regular features, and . . . I could not help sometimes fancying that it much resembled a European!"

Narratives of the Mission of George Bogle to Tibet and of the Journey of Thomas Manning to Lhasa, *ed. by Clements R. Markham* (*Trübner and Company: London, 1876*) *pp. 105–107, 108–110.*

Climbing the Mountain
of Sepulchers

Right: an engraving based on a drawing
by Robert Ker Porter of a Persian lady,
garbed in the traditional *bourkha*.

**European travelers to Persia have always been fascinated by its
ancient palaces, tombs, and monuments—relics of Persia's days
of glory some 2,500 years ago. Some of these ancient structures,
like the ruined palaces at Persepolis and Susa, are relatively
easy to visit. But others, like the cliff-side tombs at Nakshi-
Roustam, present a real challenge to the would-be explorer. In
this passage, Robert Ker Porter, a British traveler of the early
1800's, describes the novel way he gained access to them.**

"Nakshi-Roustam, or the Mountain of Sepulchers, was the next
object of my investigation. . . . The face of the mountain is almost a
perpendicular cliff. . . .

"There were no other means by which a stranger to these heights
could reach them but by the expedient of tying a rope round his waist
and some strong arms above, hauling him upward. . . . My *mehman-
dar* [servant] was at his stories and forebodings again, for tempting
such demon-wrought places. But the peasantry of this district
seemed to know better than to have fear of either *deeve* [demon] or
difficulty, and one of them more active and sinewy than the rest
managed to scramble up the perpendicular cliff, like a rat hanging
by a wall. . . . Gaining the ledge of the platform, or vestibule of
the tomb, he lowered down a rope, by which some of his nimble
companions assisted themselves in ascending. I followed the example
by fastening the rope round my waist, and by their united exertions

Left: Robert Ker Porter's drawing of himself being hauled up to view the Mountain of Sepulchers.

Right: the chief executioner at the Persian court, sketched by Ker Porter. Even the highest of the courtiers might one day find himself in his hands. Because of this, the chief executioner was treated with great respect by all.

was speedily drawn up to the place of rendezvous. . . .

"During my ascent . . . I could not but recollect the fate of half a dozen kinsmen of Darius Hystaspes [king of Persia, 521–486 B.C.], who had all perished at once in the very same expedition. Ctesias [a Greek historian] relates that this great Persian monarch 'caused a tomb to be dug for him while he yet lived, in the double mountain. But when it was completed, the Chaldean soothsayers forbid him to enter it during his life under a penalty of some terrible danger. Darius was intimidated, but some princes of his family could not resist a strong curiosity which impelled them to view its interior. They went to the mountain, and by their desire were to be drawn up by the priests who officiated there. But in the act, while they yet hung between earth and air, the sudden appearance of some serpents on the rock so terrified the people above that they let go the ropes, and the princes were dashed to pieces.'

"On this very spot, more than 2,000 years ago, the catastrophe happened. I should have read the history of this disaster at home with almost as little concern as if the people had never existed; here I was on the spot where it happened. . . . The persons seemed present with me, and I shuddered for them while I rejoiced in my own safety."

Travels in Georgia, Persia, Armenia, Ancient Babylonia, *Robert Ker Porter* (London: 1821) pp. 515–516, 520–522.

A Gift for the Shah

The British diplomat James Morier won widespread fame in the early 1800's for his amusing "fictional" accounts of life in Persia. But as this factual account shows, Morier did not have to look far to find humorous episodes for his stories.

"Mahomed Khan, the head of the king's camel artillery . . . made levies of men throughout the country for the purpose of carrying the [British Embassy's] baggage, which consisted of several carriages, looking glasses . . . and many other heavy pieces of furniture.

As the Persians have no wheeled conveyances, and as the greater part of these articles were too bulky to be loaded on camels, they were carried on the backs of men. . . . One of the modes adopted for lessening the labor of descending the steep mountains between Bushire and Shiraz was that of fastening some of the cases upon a [British] gun carriage, and permitting it to run at random down the declivities, by which contrivance most of the carriages were disabled, and of course the thing attached to them totally demolished. . . .

"The carriages which were brought as presents to the king were not put together until they reached us at Tehran. One that had been built in England on purpose for the king . . . we succeeded to render serviceable, and then the ambassador presented it to His Majesty. . . .

"It was dragged with considerable difficulty through the narrow streets and bazaars to the king's palace, where the ambassador, attended by the grand vizier, and all the principal officers of the state, were in readiness to exhibit it to the king. His Majesty walked around the carriage, examined it very minutely, admired its beauty, criticized its contrivances, and then got inside, leaving his shoes at the door and seating himself with much satisfaction upon the

Left: Portrait of James Morier from a mezzotint by S. W. Reynolds after Sir W. Boxall, R.A.

Left: Kurdish tribesmen, sketched by Morier when they visited his camp at Aberan. The man with the spear was nicknamed Bull, for his great strength.

velvet cushions. . . . Some of the secretaries of state and other personages of rank, all in their court dresses, then fastened themselves to it and dragged His Majesty backward and forward to his great delight, which he expressed by some good remarks on the conveniency of carriages and the ingenuity of Europeans, who had brought them to such perfection. The circumstance that surprised the grand vizier the most was that it could go backward as well as forward. The king kept his seat for more than half an hour, observing that there would be a very good sitting room for two. . . . However, we learned shortly after that it was put into a warehouse, where it was bricked up, where it has been ever since, and where it is likely to remain."

Left: the luxury of a Persian breakfast, an engraving based on Morier's sketch.

A Second Journey through Persia, Armenia, and Asia Minor, *James Morier (London: 1818) pp. 197–198.*

Through "Pestilential Vapors"

In the winter of 1845, the French missionaries Evarist Huc and Joseph Gabet, in company with a large merchant caravan, crossed the rugged mountain ranges guarding the northern Tibetan plateau. In this passage, Huc describes the agonizing ordeal he and his companions underwent in ascending the Bourhan-Bota Pass and Mount Chuga.

"On the 15th November, we . . . entered upon the territory of the Mongols of Tsaidam. Immediately after crossing the river of that name, we found the aspect of the country totally changed. Nature becomes all of a sudden savage and sad. . . . We stayed two days in the land of Tsaidam, feasting upon . . . some goats which the shepherds gave in exchange for some bricks of tea. The grand object with the whole caravan was to get up its strength as much as possible, with a view to the passage of the Bourhan-Bota, a mountain noted for the pestilential vapors in which, as we were informed, it is constantly enveloped.

"We started at three in the morning, and after infinite sinuosities and meanderings over this hilly country, we arrived, by nine o'clock, at the foot of the Bourhan-Bota. There the caravan halted for a moment, as if to poise its strength; everybody measured with his eyes the steep and rugged paths of the lofty ascent, gazed with anxiety at a light, thin vapor, which we were told was the pestilential vapor in question, and . . . began to clamber up the side of the mountain. Before long, the horses refused to carry their riders, and all, men as well as animals, advanced on foot, and step by step.

"By degrees, our faces grew pale, our hearts sick, and our legs incapable of supporting us. We threw ourselves on the ground, then rose again to make another effort, then once more prostrated ourselves, and again rose to stumble on some paces farther. . . . Heavens! what wretchedness it was we went through! One's strength seemed exhausted, one's head turning round, one's limbs dislocated. It was just like a thoroughly bad sea-sickness. And yet, all the while, one has to retain enough energy, not only to drag one's self on, but, moreover, to keep thrashing the animals which lie down at every step and can hardly be got to move.

"One portion of the caravan, as a measure of precaution, stopped halfway up the mountain, in a gully where the pestilential vapors, they said, were not so dense. The other portion of the caravan,

equally as a measure of precaution, exerted their most intense efforts in order to make their way right up to the top, so as to avoid being asphyxiated by that dreadful air.... We were of the number of those who ascended the Bourhan-Bota at one stretch. On reaching its summit, our lungs dilated at their ease. The descent of the mountain was mere child's-play, and we were soon able to set up our tent far from the murderous air we had encountered on the ascent....

"The passage of the Bourhan-Bota was but a sort of apprenticeship. A few days after, Mount Chuga put our strength and courage

Left: Huc and Gabet, with their escort, crossing an extremely dangerous bridge after they had left the city of Lhasa.

Right: Huc in one of the disguises he assumed for the journey, that of a Chinese merchant. Often when entering Mongol regions, he dressed as a lama.

Below left: one of Huc's carts turned over on the ice. Their Chinese driver quickly fixed it with a large stone, a few sticks, and a length of rope.

to a still more formidable test. The day's march being long and laborious, the cannon shot, our signal for departure, was heard at one o'clock in the morning....

"Mount Chuga being not very steep in the direction where we approached it, we were able to attain the summit by sunrise. Almost immediately afterward, however, the sky became thickly overcast with clouds, and the wind began to blow with a violence which grew constantly more and more intense. The opposite sides of the mountain we found so encumbered with snow that the animals were up to their girths in it; they could only advance by a series of convulsive efforts.... We marched in the very teeth of a wind so strong and so icy that it absolutely at times choked our respiration, and despite our thick furs, made us tremble lest we should be killed with the cold.... When we reached the foot of the mountain, and could use our eyes, we found that more than one face had been frozen in the descent."

Travels in Tartary, Thibet, and China, Evarist Huc Vol. 2 *trans. by William Hazlitt (Office of the National Illustrated Library: London) pp. 113–116.*

Drama in the Desert

What is it like to be the last survivors of an expedition, desperately seeking for water in a nightmare landscape of burning sand and blazing sun? This terrifying ordeal, experienced by Sven Hedin and his faithful companion Kasim in the midst of the Taklamakan Desert in 1893, is here described by the explorer himself.

"We collapsed on the slope of a dune. . . . For fully ten hours we lay silent in the sand. It was strange that we were still alive. Would we have strength enough to drag ourselves through one more night— our last one? I rose at twilight and urged Kasim to come. Hardly audible was his gasp: 'I can't go on.'

"And so I left the last remnant of the caravan behind and continued on alone. I dragged myself along, and fell. . . . I lay quiet for long periods, listening. Not a sound! The stars shone like electric torches [flashlights]. I wondered whether I was still on earth, or whether this was the valley of the shadow of death. . . After a couple of hours, I heard the swish of steps in the sand, and saw a phantom stagger and struggle to my side.

" 'Is that you, Kasim?' I whispered.

Below left: a wild yak that charged Hedin's dogs on his arduous journey.

Below: the outcome of the encounter: Hedin's photograph of the yak after it had been shot. It was subsequently cut up and provided a good supply of fresh meat for the next few days.

176

" 'Yes, sir.'

" 'Come! We have not far to go!'

"Heartened by our reunion, we struggled on. . . . We were like
sleepwalkers, but still we fought for our lives. Suddenly, Kasim
grabbed my arm and pointed downward at the sand. There were
distinct tracks of human beings! In a twinkling we were wide awake.
. . . Kasim bent down, examined the prints, and gasped: 'It is our
own trail!' In our listless, somnolent state, we had described a circle
without knowing it. That was enough for a while. We could not
endure any more. We collapsed on the trail and fell asleep.

"When the new day dawned on May 5, we rose heavily and with
difficulty. Kasim looked terrible. His tongue was white and swollen,
his lips blue, his cheeks were hollow, and his eyes had a dying,
glassy lustre. . . . The sun rose. From the top of a dune, where
nothing obstructed the view toward the east, we noticed that the
horizon, which for two weeks had revealed a row of yellow sawteeth,
now disclosed an absolutely even, dark green line. We stopped short,
as though petrified, and exclaimed simultaneously: 'The forest!'
And I added: 'The Khotan-daria [Khotan River]! Water!'

"Again we collected what little strength we had left and struggled
along eastward. . . . The dark green line grew, the dunes diminished,
stopped altogether, and were replaced by level soft ground. We were
but a few hundred yards from the forest. . . . Kasim lay on his back.
He looked as if he were going to die. The river *must* be quite near. . . .
I urged Kasim to accompany me to the river to drink. He signaled
with his hand that he could not rise. . . .

"Alone I pulled myself along through the forest. Thickets of
thorny bushes and dry fallen branches obstructed my way. I tore
my thin clothes and scratched my hands, but gradually I worked my
way through. . . . The forest ended abruptly, as though burnt by a

Above: Hedin's drawing of his
agonizing search for water in the
midst of the Taklamakan Desert.

Below: attracted by the sound of a duck,
he found a pool of water in the dry bed
of the Khotan River, which saved his
life and that of his servant Kasim.

Drama in the Desert

fire. I found myself on the edge of . . . the river bed of the Khotan-daria. And it was dry, as dry as the sandy desert behind me!

"Was I to die of thirst in the very bed of the river, after having fought my way so successfully to its bank? No! I was not going to lie down and die without first crossing the Khotan-daria and assuring myself that the whole bed was dry, and that all hope was irretrievably gone. . . .

"I walked as though led by an invisible hand. . . . A light haze floated over the desolate landscape. I had gone about one mile when the outlines of the forest on the eastern shore appeared below the moon. . . . The bed still remained as dry as before. It was not far to the shore where I must lie down and die. My life hung by a hair.

"Suddenly I started, and stopped short. A water bird, a wild duck or goose, rose on whirring wings, and I heard a splash. The next moment, I stood on the edge of a pool seventy feet long and fifteen feet wide! In the silent night I thanked God for my miraculous deliverance."

My Life as an Explorer, *Sven Hedin (Cassell and Company: London, New York, Toronto, and Melbourne, 1926) pp. 136–140.*

Above: a mendicant lama whom Hedin met on the Tibetan plateau. Pilgrims thought of these holy beggars as mediators between the gods and men.

Left: the forest fire that Hedin and Kasim set to attract the attention of passing nomads after their companions and animals had died of thirst.

Clash on the Guru Plain

The British "massacre" of Tibetan troops on the Guru Plain in 1904 created a storm of controversy. The leader of the British expedition, Francis Younghusband, was bitterly criticized for his handling of the affair. In this passage, Younghusband defends himself by describing what actually occurred at Guru on that tragic day.

"As we advanced across an almost level gravelly plain, we came in sight of the Tibetan position in a series of *sangars* [barricades] on a ridge. At 1,000 yards' distance we halted, and awaited the arrival of the Tibetans for our last palaver [talk]. They rode up briskly with a little cavalcade, and we all dismounted, set out rugs and coats on the ground, and sat down for the final discussion. I reiterated the same old statement—that we had no wish or intention of fighting if we were not opposed, but that we must advance to Gyantse. If they did not obstruct our progress or did not attack us, we would not attack them. But advance we must, for we had found it impossible to negotiate anywhere else. They replied with the request . . . that we must go back to Yatung, and they would negotiate there. They said these were their instructions from Lhasa. . . .

Above: Younghusband's expedition with part of the mule train. He left India with 7,000 mules and 5,000 bullocks.

Left: the last meeting, when the Lhasa general came to Younghusband's tent for a final talk before the Guru battle.

Clash on the Guru Plain

Above: some of the Tibetan dead photographed as they had fallen after the battle-turned-massacre at Guru.

Below: a photograph of a group of Younghusband's British officers in Tibet, with a sepoy standing in front.

"There was no possible reasoning with such people. They had such overweening confidence in their Lama's powers. How *could* anyone dare to resist the orders of the Great Lama? Surely lightning would descend from heaven or the earth open up and destroy anyone who had such temerity! I pointed to our troops, now ready deployed for action. I said that . . . I would give them a quarter of an hour . . . to make up their minds. After that interval, General Macdonald would advance, and if the Tibetans had not already left their positions blocking our line of advance, he would expel them by force. . . .

"The generals and their following returned to their camp. The quarter of an hour of grace elapsed. And now the great moment had arrived. But I wished still to give them just one last chance, in the hope that at the eleventh hour, and at the fifty-ninth minute of the eleventh hour, they might change their minds. I therefore asked General Macdonald to order his men not to fire upon the Tibetans until the Tibetans first fired on them. . . .

"It was the last and final effort to carry out our object without the shedding of blood. The troops responded with admirable discipline to the call. They steadily advanced across the plain and up the hillside to the Tibetan lines, expecting at any moment that from behind the sangars a destructive volley might be opened upon them. . . . The Tibetans on their side showed great indecision. They also had apparently received orders not to fire first, and the whole affair seemed likely to end in comedy rather than in the tragedy which actually followed. . . .

"The Tibetans were streaming away from their position along the ridge, and had even begun to leave their post on the road. Then a change came. The Lhasa general, or possibly the monks, recalled the men to their post, and an officer reported to General Macdonald that though surrounded by our troops, they refused to retreat; they were not fighting, but they would not leave the wall they had built across the road. General Macdonald and I had a consultation together, and agreed that in these circumstances the only thing to do was to disarm them and let them go. We rode together to the spot, and found the Tibetans huddled together like a flock of sheep behind the wall. . . . Our sepoys [Indian troops] were actually standing up to the wall, with their rifles pointing over at the Tibetans within a few feet of them. And the Lhasa general himself with his staff was on *our* side of the wall, in among our sepoys.

Pango kaling gate

Gold

Chains with Bells

Connected with another small Chaiten up here

End of Rocky Ridge descending from Pota Ca

Wall.

British Troops escorting a British Commissioner entering Lhasa for the 1st time. 4.VIII.'04

2 Coys Royal Fusiliers passing through the Pango Ling

Above: a photograph showing the Potala of Lhasa and the route along which the British marched as they entered the city.

Left: a drawing by N. Rybot, showing the gate through which the British force marched triumphantly into Lhasa.

"He had, of course, completely lost his head. . . . And when, after a pause, the disarmament was actually commenced, he threw himself upon a sepoy, drew a revolver, and shot the sepoy in the jaw. . . . Not, I think, with any deliberate intention, but from sheer inanity, the signal had now been given. Other Tibetan shots immediately followed. Simultaneously, volleys from our own troops rang out. . . . For just one single instant, the Tibetans, by a concerted and concentrated rush, might have broken our thin line. . . . But that instant passed in a flash. Before a few seconds were over, rifles and guns were dealing the deadliest destruction on them in their huddled masses. The Lhasa general himself was killed at the start, and in a few minutes the whole affair was over. The plain was strewn with dead Tibetans. . . .

"It was a terrible and ghastly business, but it was not fair for an English statesman to call it a massacre of 'unarmed men,' for photographs testify that the Tibetans were all armed. And looking back now, I do not see how it could possibly have been avoided."

India and Tibet, *Francis Younghusband* (*John Murray: London, 1910*) *pp. 174–178.*

The Explorers

ANDRADE, FATHER ANTONIO DE
1580–1634   Portugal
1624: Disguised as a Hindu pilgrim,
traveled from Delhi, in northern India,
to Tsaparang, in western Tibet; one of
the first Europeans to penetrate deep
into the Himalaya. Returned to India.
1625: Went back to Tsaparang with
several other Jesuits to build a mission.
1629: Recalled to India to become the
Jesuit superior at Goa.
See map on page 82.

**AZEVADO, FATHER FRANCISCO
DE**
1578–1660   Portugal
1631: At the request of Father Andrade,
traveled from India to Leh, in Kashmir,
where he persuaded the local ruler to
free his Christian slaves and permit
the reopening of the Tsaparang mission.
See map on page 82.

BERING, VITUS
1680–1741   Denmark
1725–1729: For Peter the Great,
headed an expedition to discover
whether Asia and North America were
separated by water. Traveled to
Kamchatka, then built boats and
sailed up the east coast of the
peninsula as far as latitude 67° 18′ N.
Turned back for fear of bad weather
after determining that there was a
strait between the two continents.
1741: Died of scurvy after a second
expedition lasting several years. In
the course of this expedition, he had
sailed southeast from Kamchatka
sighting the Alaskan coast and
exploring the Aleutian Islands. Bering
Island, Bering Strait, and the Bering
Sea are named for him.
See map on page 48.

BOGLE, GEORGE
1746–1781   Scotland
1770: Arrived in Calcutta as a junior
officer in the East India Company.
1774–1775: Chosen by Warren Hastings
to be the first British envoy to Tibet.
Traveled to Tashilhumpo, in eastern
Tibet. Failed to win Lhasa authorities'
agreement to establish Anglo-Tibetan
trade links, but won the enduring
friendship of the Panchen Lama.

1781: Died suddenly of a fever in India.
See map on page 116.

CABRAL, FATHER JOAO
1599–1669   Portugal
1626–1628: With Father Cacella
traveled from India to Shigatse, in
eastern Tibet, becoming the first
Europeans to visit Bhutan. Founded a
mission at Shigatse.
1628: Became the first European to
travel through Nepal, stopping
at its capital Katmandu.
1631: Made final journey to Shigatse.
See map on page 82.

CACELLA, FATHER ESTEVAO
1585–1630   Portugal
1626–1627: Traveled with Father
Cabral from India to Tibet and
founded a mission at Shigatse.
1628–1630: Attempted to reach the
Tsaparang mission, but was forced back
by heavy snows. Made his way to India,
where he joined Cabral. Died soon
after returning to Shigatse.
See map on page 82.

CHANCELLOR, RICHARD
(?)–1556   England
1553: Pilot-general of the English
expedition that sailed in search of a
Northeast Passage to Cathay (China).
Reached the shores of northern
Russia, then made his way south to
Moscow, where he laid the foundations
of future Anglo-Russian trade.
1556: Drowned off the coast of
Scotland on his return from a second
expedition to Russia.
See map on page 48.

CHRISTIE, CHARLES
(?)–1812   England
1810: With Henry Pottinger, explored
the southern portion of what is now
Pakistan. Alone, journeyed to
Herat before rejoining Pottinger in
Persia.
1812: Was killed while assisting
the Persians in their war
against Russia.
See map on page 137.

DE GOES, FATHER BENTO
1562–1607   Portugal

1603–1607: Sent by the Jesuits at Goa
to discover whether Cathay and China
were identical. Traveled north from
India to Kabul, in Afghanistan, and
thence eastward through Chinese
Turkestan to Suchow at the western
end of the Gobi Desert. From there, got
in touch with the Jesuit superior at
Peking, but died soon after receiving
the reply that finally proved that China
and Cathay were one and the same.
See map on page 82.

DESHNEF, SEMEN IVANOVICH
1605(?)–1673(?)   Russia
1648–1649: Commanded a Cossack
fleet that sailed along the Kolyma River
to the East Siberian Sea and thence
along the coast, rounding the extreme
northeastern shores of Asia.
Was the first to sail through
the Bering Strait and possibly down the
coast of the Kamchatka Peninsula.
See map on page 48.

DESIDERI, FATHER IPPOLITO
1684–1733   Italy
1714–1716: With Father Freyre,
traveled through Kashmir to Leh,
and thence eastward to Lhasa,
becoming the first Europeans to see
Mount Kailas and the first to travel the
length of the Himalaya. In Lhasa, made
a study of Tibetan language, customs,
religion.
1721: Recalled from Tibet when the
pope decided that Capuchin
missionaries should work in Lhasa.
See map on page 82.

D'ORVILLE, FATHER ALBERT
1621–1662   Belgium
1661–1662: With Father Grueber,
traveled from Peking to Lhasa,
becoming the first Europeans to reach
the Tibetan capital from China. Left
Lhasa and traveled to Katmandu,
Nepal. Worn out by his travels, died
at Agra, India.
See map on page 82.

FERRIER, J. P.
dates unknown   France
1845: Having served some years as an
advisor to the Persian army, set out
to explore Afghanistan. Traveled to

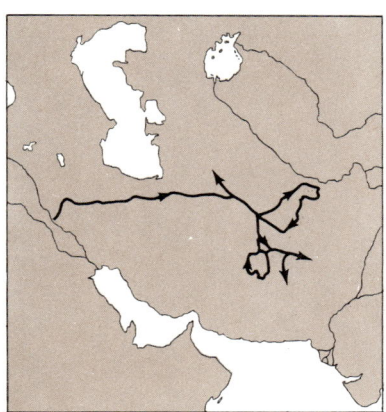

Herat, and thence to southeastern Afghanistan, but was turned back before he could reach his ultimate destination, northern India.

FREYRE, FATHER EMANUEL
1679–(?)   Portugal
1715–1716: With Father Desideri, traveled to Leh, and thence to Lhasa, from northern India. Returned alone to India by way of Nepal.
See map on page 82.

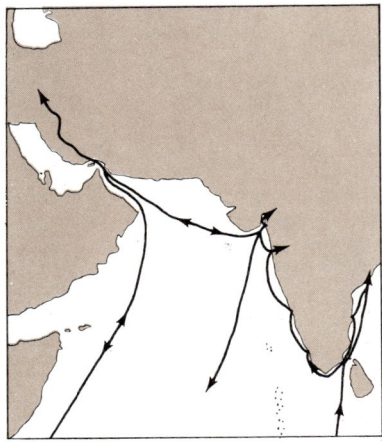

FRYER, JOHN
1650(?)–1733   England
1672–1682: Traveled widely in India and Persia in the interests of the English East India Company.

GABET, FATHER JOSEPH
dates unknown   France
1844–1846: With Abbé Huc, traveled from Peking through Inner Mongolia, central China, and Tibet, to Lhasa, and then back to China.
See map on page 82.

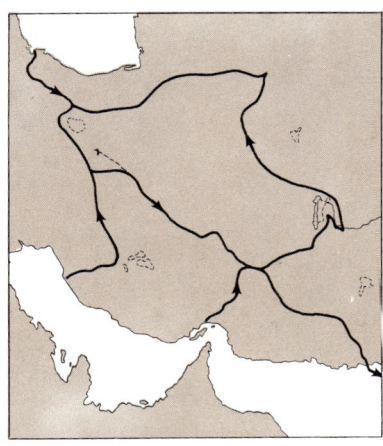

GOLDSMID, SIR FREDERICK
1818–1908   England
1864–1872: Headed expeditions that explored hitherto unmapped territories in Baluchistan (part of present-day Pakistan), Afghanistan, and Persia.

GRUEBER, FATHER JOHN
1623–1680   Austria
1661–1662: With Father D'Orville, traveled from Peking to Lhasa, becoming one of the first Europeans to reach the Tibetan capital from China. Left Lhasa and traveled to Katmandu, Nepal.
1662: Reached Agra, India, where D'Orville died. Continued on alone through Persia, and Turkey to Rome.
See map on page 82.

HANWAY, JONAS
1712–1786   England
1743: Journeyed to Russia to trade.
1743–1745: Traveled from Russia, via the Caspian Sea, to the Persian city of Astrabad, where he was robbed by

Qajar rebels. Visited the shah at Hamadan, won compensation for his stolen goods at Astrabad, and returned to England.

HEARSEY, HYDER YOUNG
1782–1840   England
1812: With William Moorcroft, crossed the Himalaya from the direction of India and explored western Tibet, becoming the first Englishmen to see Mount Kailas and Lake Manasarowar. Returned to India by way of Nepal.
See map on page 116.

HEDIN, SVEN ANDERS
1865–1952   Sweden
1890–1891: Traveled from Persia to Kashgar and crossed the Tien Shan.
1893–1897: Set out from Kashgar and entered Taklamakan Desert, where most of his expedition died from thirst. Returned to Kashgar, organized a new expedition, and carried out extensive explorations in the Taklamakan before making his way to Peking and Siberia.
1899–1902: Traveled widely in Chinese Turkestan and eastern Tibet.
1906–1908: Carried out explorations between Leh and Shigatse in Tibet.

Discovered a large range of mountains lying parallel to the Himalaya, and located the source of the Indus and Tsangpo rivers.
1927–1933: Led a major scientific expedition into Inner Mongolia and Sinkiang.
1933–1935: Surveyed part of the ancient Silk Road in Central Asia.
See map on page 150.

HUC, ABBÉ EVARIST
1813–1860   France
1829: Arrived in China to begin missionary work.
1844–1846: With Joseph Gabet, set out from Peking and traveled westward through the plains of Inner Mongolia, then south through the Ordos Desert and into Tibet. Reached Lhasa, but was forced to leave after three months by the Chinese ambassador. Returned to eastern China.
See map on page 82.

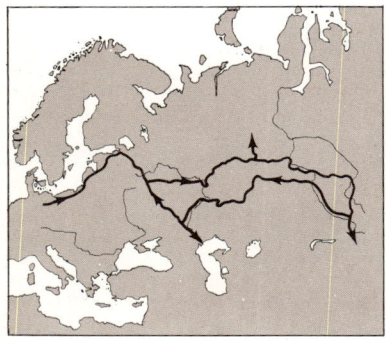

HUMBOLDT, ALEXANDER VON
1769–1859   Germany
1799–1803: Carried out scientific explorations in South America.
1829: For the Russian government, made an expedition into Siberia. Visited Tobolsk, then traveled east reaching the Altai Mountains and the Dzungaria Desert. Before returning to Moscow, he traveled down the Volga to the Caspian Sea.

JENKINSON, ANTONY
(?)–1611   England
1557: Sailed to Russia as merchant-ambassador for the Muscovy Company.
1558: In search of Cathay, sailed down the Volga to Astrakhan, then eastward across the Caspian Sea. Got as far as Bukhara before turning back.
1561–1564: Again for the Muscovy Company, sailed down the Volga to the Caspian, then down the Caspian's west coast to northern Persia. Visited the shah at Qazvin and laid the foundations for future Anglo-Persian trade.
1566: Again visited Russia and gained great trading privileges for England.

1571: Made a final trip to Russia as England's ambassador to the czar.
See maps on pages 48 and 137.

KINTUP
dates unknown   Sikkim
1880–1884: In the service of the British Survey Corps, set out from India with a Mongolian lama to explore the Tsangpo River in southern Tibet. Was sold to a Tibetan lama, but eventually managed to escape and carry out his mission on the Tsangpo.
See map on page 116.

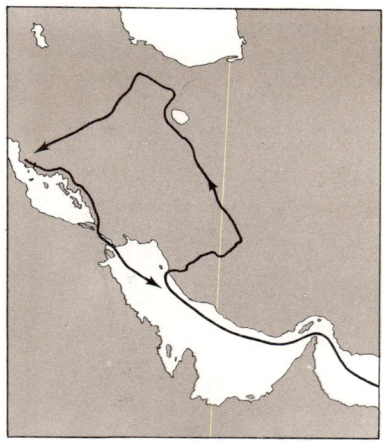

MALCOLM, SIR JOHN
1769–1833   Scotland
1783: Arrived in India as a junior officer in the East India Company's army.
1800: Sent to Persia to arrange a political and commercial treaty.
1808: Headed another mission to Persia.
1810: Third diplomatic mission to Persia. Sent Christie and Pottinger to explore region between India and Persia.

MANNING, THOMAS
1772–1840   England
1807–1810: Worked for the English East India Company in Canton, China.
1811: Traveled from India, through Bhutan, to Lhasa. Though acting in an unofficial capacity, he secured an interview with the Dalai Lama before returning to India.
See map on page 116.

MOORCROFT, WILLIAM
1765–1825   England
1812: With Hyder Young Hearsey, crossed the Himalaya from India and explored western Tibet, becoming the first Englishmen to see Mount Kailas and Lake Manasarowar. Returned to India by way of Nepal.
1819–1825: With a geologist of the East India Company, explored Ladakh,

Baltistan (northwest of Ladakh), and western Chinese Turkestan. Was killed by local tribesmen, south of Bukhara.
See map on page 116.

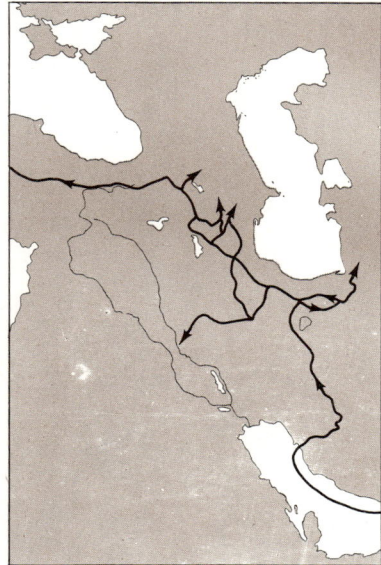

MORIER, JAMES
1780(?)–1849   England
1808–1809: Served as secretary to the British mission at Teheran, Persia.
1809–1810: Accompanied Persian ambassador to England and back.
1814: Became head of the British embassy at Teheran.

NEWBERRY, JOHN
(?)–1584   England
1581–1582: Traveled from the eastern Mediterranean to the Euphrates River, and thence south through Persia to the Persian Gulf. Visited Hormuz, Bandar Abbas, Isfahan, Shiraz, and Tabriz, becoming the first Englishman to traverse Persia.
1583: Led a trading expedition from Aleppo to Hormuz, where he and his companions were captured by the Portuguese and sent to Goa. Was released, but died on the way back to England.
See map on page 137.

POTTINGER, SIR HENRY
1789–1856   England
1810: With Charles Christie, explored the southern portion of what is now Pakistan. Alone, proceeded westward through southern Persia before rejoining Christie at Isfahan.
See map on page 137.

POYARKOV, VASILIY DANILOVICH
dates unknown   Russia

1643–1646: Led a party of 130 Cossacks from Yakutsk, on the Lena River in Siberia, southeast to the Amur River. Followed the river to its mouth, battling local tribes along the way. Credited with the discovery and first navigation of the Amur.
See map on page 48.

PRZHEVALSKI, NIKOLAI MIKHAILOVICH
1839–1888   Russia
1870–1873: Traveled from northeastern Mongolia to Peking, and thence across the Ordos Desert to the Koko Nor. Returned to Mongolia via same route.
1876–1877: Crossed the Tien Shan and explored the Tarim River and Lop Nor region. Proceeded south and discovered the Altyn Tagh mountain range.
1879–1880: Traveled south over the Dzungaria Desert to Hami, then crossed the Altyn Tagh range into Tibet. Was turned back by the Tibetan authorities when only 170 miles from Lhasa.
1883–1885: Traveled from northeastern Mongolia across the Ordos, and explored the source of the Hwang Ho in the Tibetan plateau. Turned northwest, crossing the Altyn Tagh into the Taklamakan Desert, and crossed the Tien Shan.
1888: Died at Karakul, near Bukhara, at the start of his fifth expedition.
See map on page 150.

SEMENOV, PETER
1827–1914   Russia
1856–1859: Crossed the Tien Shan range from the north. Also traversed the Dzungaria Desert and explored the Altai Mountains.
1888: Led an expedition through the region east of the Caspian Sea and on into Chinese province of Sinkiang.

SHERLEY, SIR ROBERT
1581(?)–1628   England
1599: With Sir Anthony Sherley, accompanied party of Englishmen to Persia.
1599–1608: Advised Shah Abbas on

modern military techniques. Played a distinguished role in Persia's wars against the Turks. Married a Persian princess.
1609–1616: Traveled through Europe as the shah's envoy. Returned to Persia.
1616–1627: Again visited the courts of Europe on the shah's behalf.
1628: Died soon after returning to Persia and being rejected by the shah.
See map on page 137.

SINGH, KISHEN
1842(?)–1921   India
1871–1872: In the service of the British Survey Corps, traveled to Shigatse and the Tengri Nor in western Tibet. Returned to India by way of Lhasa.
1878–1882: From Lhasa, traveled northeast through Tibet and into central China, reaching Tunhwang before making his way back to India.
See map on page 116.

SINGH, NAIN
(?)–1882   India
1865–1866: In the service of the British Survey Corps, traveled to eastern Tibet via Nepal, visiting Tashilhumpo before going on to Lhasa. Plotted exact location of Lhasa, and made an elaborate survey of the surrounding area.
1867: Explored the Thok-Jalung gold mines in western Tibet.
1874–1875: Thoroughly explored region between Leh, in Ladakh, and Lhasa, discovering hitherto unmapped lakes, rivers, and mountains, before returning to India.
See map on page 116.

STEIN, SIR AUREL
1862–1943   England
1900–1901: Carried out a reconnaissance of the Pamirs, the Hindu Kush, and the western Taklamakan Desert, visiting Khotan, Kashgar, Samarkand.
1906–1908: Headed an archaeological expedition that traveled from the Pamirs and the Hindu Kush eastward into the Taklamakan, exploring and excavating ancient cities. At Tunhwang, at the western end of the Gobi, he explored the famous "Caves of the Thousand Buddhas," and returned to England with a cargo of manuscripts and art treasures.
1913–1914: Traveled north through the Karakoram range to Kashgar, and thence to Khotan. From there he made his way east to Lop Nor and the Nan Shan range before returning to Kashgar.
1915–1916: Traveled from Kashgar westward through the Pamirs and the Hindu Kush to Bukhara and Persia.
See map on page 159.

SYKES, SIR PERCY
1867–1945   England

1893: Traveled from Astrabad to Meshed and thence southwest across Persia to Kerman, Shiraz, and the Persian Gulf.
1893–1894: Explored region between Chahrar on the Gulf of Oman, and Kerman, and proceeded north to the Caspian Sea.
1894: Traveled south from the Caspian, exploring central and southern Persia.
1897–1901: Explored region between Bandar Abbas and Chahrar, then traveled northwest to Kerman.
1902–1906: Explored regions southeast and northeast of Kerman.
1906–1910: Explored territory between Astrabad and Meshed.
1915–1919: Carried out survey expeditions along the coast of the Gulf of Oman; between Kerman and Bandar Abbas; between Bushire and Isfahan; between Baghdad and Teheran; along the border between Persia and Afghanistan; and between the Caspian and the Hindu Kush.
See map on page 137.

TURNER, SAMUEL
1749–1802   England
1783–1784: Headed a British diplomatic mission to Tibet, and negotiated with the Panchen Lama's regent at Tashilhumpo. Returned to India via Bhutan.
See map on page 116.

YERMAK, TIMOFEYEVICH
1540–1584   Russia
1577: With his men, fled to the Urals to escape the czar's armies, and was hired by Maxim Stroganov to drive the Mongols out of western Siberia.
1578–1582: Led his men across the Urals and thence eastward to the Mongol stronghold of Sibir on the Irtysh River. Captured Sibir and sent word of the conquest to Czar Ivan IV.
1584: Was drowned in the Irtysh River while fleeing from a band of Mongol warriors.
See map on page 48.

YOUNGHUSBAND, SIR FRANCIS
1863–1942   England
1886: Won an appointment to Peking and visited Manchuria.
1887: Traveled from Peking across the Gobi and the Nomin Gobi deserts to the Karlik Tagh, and then to Kashgar and Yarkand. Crossed the Karakorams via the Mustagh Pass, and then rejoined his regiment in India.
1889–1895: Made a number of exploratory journeys into the mountains northwest of India.
1903–1904: Headed the British expedition that fought its way to Lhasa and forced the Tibetan authorities to agree to a treaty with Britain.
See map on page 150.

Glossary

(For words not commonly used in English, the foreign derivation is given.)

argol: (Mongolian) Dried cow dung used as fuel by the nomads of Central Asia.

bazaar: (Persian) A marketplace or shopping quarter, often roofed over, and occupying a single, narrow street, or a series of streets and squares.

bourkha: (Persian) Persian lady's all-enveloping tent-like garment.

boyar: (Russian) A member of a powerful strata of Russia's landowning aristocrats which wielded immense power before Peter the Great abolished the title.

Buddhism: The religion founded by Siddhartha Gautama, a prince born in what is now Nepal about 563 B.C. Gautama's teachings earned him the title *Buddha*, meaning "the enlightened one." He stressed self-knowledge, self-discipline, and loving kindness as the way to perfect peace. Buddha's followers spread his teachings throughout the East, and today there are more than 240 million practicing Buddhists in India, Tibet, China, Japan and parts of Southeast Asia.

Capuchins: Members of a Roman Catholic order of friars founded in 1528. The Capuchins form a branch of the Order of Saint Francis, and take their name from the pointed hood, or *capuche,* that is part of their habit. The Capuchins were among the most active Catholic missionaries of the 1600's and 1700's.

caravan: A long train of people and pack animals that travels through wild or barren country. In the days before mechanized transportation, caravans consisting of as many as 5,000 camels used to carry goods from China, India, and Persia to Mediterranean markets for shipment to Europe.

Cossacks: Originally runaway serfs and outlaws from Russia, Poland, and Turkey, who banded together in the 1400's and roamed the southwestern open steppe. They soon became known far and wide for their wild and reckless way of life. The word *cossack* originally meant "free laborer," but soon came to be applied to those who escaped from society to find refuge on the steppes. A fiercely independent people, the Cossacks nevertheless fought for the czars, and eventually formed elite corps in the czars' armies. Many Cossacks were killed or deported after the civil war of 1918—1920 which followed the Bolshevik Revolution.

czar: The title used by the emperors of Russia. The word comes from the term *Caesar,* the name used by the Roman emperors. Ivan IV (Ivan the Terrible) was the first Russian ruler to adopt the title, in 1547.

Dalai Lama: The title of the supreme ruler of Tibet until 1959, when the Chinese Communists crushed a Tibetan revolt against Chinese domination. Both the spiritual and the temporal leader of his people, the Dalai Lama has traditionally been regarded as the reincarnation (reborn soul) of every previous Dalai Lama, going back to Avalokitesvara, the patron saint of all Tibetans. The present (14th) Dalai Lama lives in exile in India.

East India Company (English): An organization of English merchants founded in 1600 to exploit trading possibilities in the East Indies. Having established trading posts in India, the Company extended its influence there as the result of the disintegration of the Mogul Empire in the 1700's. After the restriction of France, the last of its major European competitors in India, to several small trading centers in 1763, the Company ruled supreme on the subcontinent until 1858, when the British government took over the the job of ruling India.

Eastern Orthodox churches: The major Christian churches of Russia, Greece, and parts of western Asia. Individually, these churches are usually called by their national names, such as the Russian Orthodox Church and the Greek Orthodox Church. A dispute over the text of the Nicene-Constantinopolitan creed, and the issue of the Pope's authority over all Christian churches led the Eastern Orthodox churches to break away from the *western* (Roman Catholic) church in 1054. Due to immigration, mostly by Greeks and Russians in the 1900's, Britain is now the home of about 250,000 members of the Eastern churches.

fakir: (Arabic) A Moslem or Hindu who practices self-denial as part of his religion. Fakirs usually live on charity and spend most of their lives in religious contemplation. Some can actually perform such feats of will power as walking on hot coals.

Golden Horde: The army of fierce, hard-riding Tartars and Mongols that swept into eastern Europe in the 1200's, and established dominion over Russia. Ivan III cast off the Horde's yoke in 1480.

Great Wall of China: The longest fortified wall ever built. It stretches from Shanhaikuan on the eastern coast into the deserts of northwestern China. The Wall was linked together around 200 B.C. by connecting older walls, and has been expanded and repaired since. Its purpose was to keep out marauding northern tribes. Built of earth, brick and stone, it averages 30 feet in height, with watchtowers averaging 40 feet.

harem: (Arabic) The part of the house set aside for the women of the family in some Moslem countries. The word also refers to the women who live in this part of the house. The harem has become identified with Moslem life because the Koran (Moslem scriptures) permits Moslem men to marry four wives and keep numerous concubines.

icon: (Greek) An image of a holy person, such as Christ or the Virgin Mary, represented in painting, enamel, or mosaic. Such holy images have traditionally formed an essential part of worship in the Eastern Orthodox churches.

Jesuits: Members of a Roman Catholic Order called the Society of Jesus, established in 1534 by Saint Ignatius Loyola. The Jesuits are considered to be among the most scholarly of Catholic educators, and since their foundation have played a leading role in missionary work throughout the world.

khan: (Turkic) A term first used by the Turks and Mongols in the A.D. 500's to mean "ruler." Later came to be applied to ranking dignitaries throughout Central Asia. Today, a term of respect in such countries as India, Persia, Afghanistan, and Pakistan.

khanate: (Turkic) A princedom, or area ruled by a khan.

Kremlin: The old fortified center of Moscow. Inside its 1½-mile-long walls stand several ornate cathedrals and the Grand Kremlin Palace, where the Supreme Soviet, Russia's parliament, meets. Just outside the Kremlin is Red Square, site of the yearly parades held on the anniversary of the Bolshevik Revolution.

lama: (Tibetan) A priest or monk of the Lamaist religion, the form of Buddhism practiced in Tibet and Mongolia.

Manchu: The name of the Manchurian people who conquered China in the 1600's. The Manchus set up a dynasty called the Ch'ing Dynasty, which ruled China until 1912, when the ruling Manchu emperor was overthrown.

mead: An alcoholic drink made from fermented honey and water.

Mogul: The Indian version of the word "Mongol." The term came to be applied to the vast Indian empire ruled by the descendants of Babar, a conqueror who invaded India in 1526. The Mogul dynasty ruled much of India until the 1700's.

Mongols: Originally, a group of nomadic people living in loosely organized tribes in Mongolia, Manchuria, and Siberia. In the early 1200's, these tribes united under a Mongol chieftain named Temujin (later known as Genghis Khan), and began a series of extensive conquests in Asia. By the mid-1200's the Mongols were the overlords of the biggest land empire in history. It stretched unbroken from the shores of China's Yellow Sea to the borders of eastern Europe. But the mighty empire built by Genghis Khan and his successors, Ogotai and Kublai Khan, lasted only until the 1300's, when it broke up into numerous warring factions.

Moslems: Believers in the religion founded by the Arab prophet Mohammed in the A.D. 600's. The term *Moslem* comes from an Arabic word meaning "one who submits" (to God). After Mohammed's death, the Moslems, who were Arabs, began to spread their religion beyond Arabia. Eventually it stretched from the Atlantic to the borders of China. The Moslems preserved much of the knowledge of the ancient world which helped lay the foundations of Western culture. Today, there are some 538 million Moslems in the world.

mosque: (Arabic) A Moslem house of worship. Many mosques have ornate pointed domes, several minarets (towers from which people are called to prayer), and large open courtyards.

Muscovy Company: The organization of English merchants that pioneered England's first trade relations with Russia and Persia in the 1500's. The association (sometimes also called the Russia Company) was founded in 1552 for the purpose of seeking a Northeast Passage to Cathay (China). The Company received its Royal Charter in 1555.

nirvana: In the Buddhist religion, the attainment of freedom from passion, hatred, and delusion. This state of "blessed oblivion," or passionless peace, is possible only when the individual has achieved perfect self-discipline, unselfishness, knowledge, and enlightenment.

Panchen Lama: The second-highest-ranking lama in Tibet. The position was created in the 1600's by the Fifth Dalai Lama for his beloved tutor Lobsang Ch'osgyi. Later Panchen Lamas were chosen, like the Dalai Lamas, on the basis of mystical signs. In 1959, when the Chinese Communists forced the 14th Dalai Lama to flee Tibet, they installed the Panchen Lama as a puppet ruler, but he, too, was stripped of his powers in 1964.

patriarch: The term used by the early Christians to honor the bishops of the most important churches. Today, the title is mainly applied to the heads of the various Eastern Orthodox churches, such as the chief bishops of the Greek Orthodox and the Russian Orthodox churches.

Potala: The palace and lamasery of the Dalai Lama in the Tibetan capital of Lhasa. Built in the mid-1600's by the Fifth Dalai Lama, the Potala rises steeply from a hill overlooking the city. Many of its 1,000 rooms are filled with Tibetan art treasures.

prayer wheel: a wheel or cylinder inscribed with, or containing a prayer, and hung in a place of worship. In Tibet, these devices—which can be turned by hand, by the wind, or by a watermill—often contain the sacred prayer *Om mani padme hum* ("Oh, the jewel in the lotus"). Turning the wheel is thought to have the same effect as repeating the prayer.

pundit: (Hindi) A wise or learned man. Indian surveyors employed by the British Survey Corps were called "pundit-explorers" because they were highly trained technicians as well as venturers into unknown territory.

purdah: (Persian) The Moslem practice of keeping women heavily veiled or in strict seclusion, so that only their immediate family may see them.

reincarnation: In the Buddhist religion, the belief that the soul is reborn in a new body after death. According to this belief, the soul passes from one body to another until it is pure enough to attain nirvana, "the blessed oblivion," and is free from the need for any further reincarnations.

sepoy: (Persian) A native of India employed as a soldier in the army of a European power.

serai: (Turkish) A desert inn or way-station at which weary merchants and travelers could find warmth, food, and shelter after a long day's march.

Silk Road: The route traditionally used by caravan merchants to bring silk and other luxury goods from China across the deserts of Central Asia to the markets of the Middle East.

sledge: A large, sturdy vehicle with low runners used for traveling swiftly over ice and snow. A sleigh.

steppes: (Russian) The great expanses of grassy plains that stretch from the Ukraine region of southern Russia to the Altai Mountains of Siberia.

Tartars: A powerful nomadic tribe of central Asia who were defeated by the Mongols in the late 1100's. The victorious Mongols adopted the name of their vanquished foe and were thus known to the outside world during the great days of the Mongol Empire. In more recent times, the term *Tartar* has been generally used in reference to the peoples of Mongolia and southern U.S.S.R.

Tartary: The name once given to the vast region ruled by the Mongols and Tartars. The region, lying outside the Great Wall of China, included present-day northern China, Mongolia, Sinkiang, and southern U.S.S.R.

tundra: The low, swampy plains lying around the Arctic Ocean in northern Eurasia and North America. Except for a few feet near the surface, tundra remains frozen even in summer.

ukase: (Russian) An order, edict, or command issued by the czar.

Index

Picture Credits

Listed below are the sources of all the illustrations in this book. To identify the source of a particular illustration, first find the relevant page on the diagram opposite. The number in black in the appropriate position on that page refers to the credit as listed below.

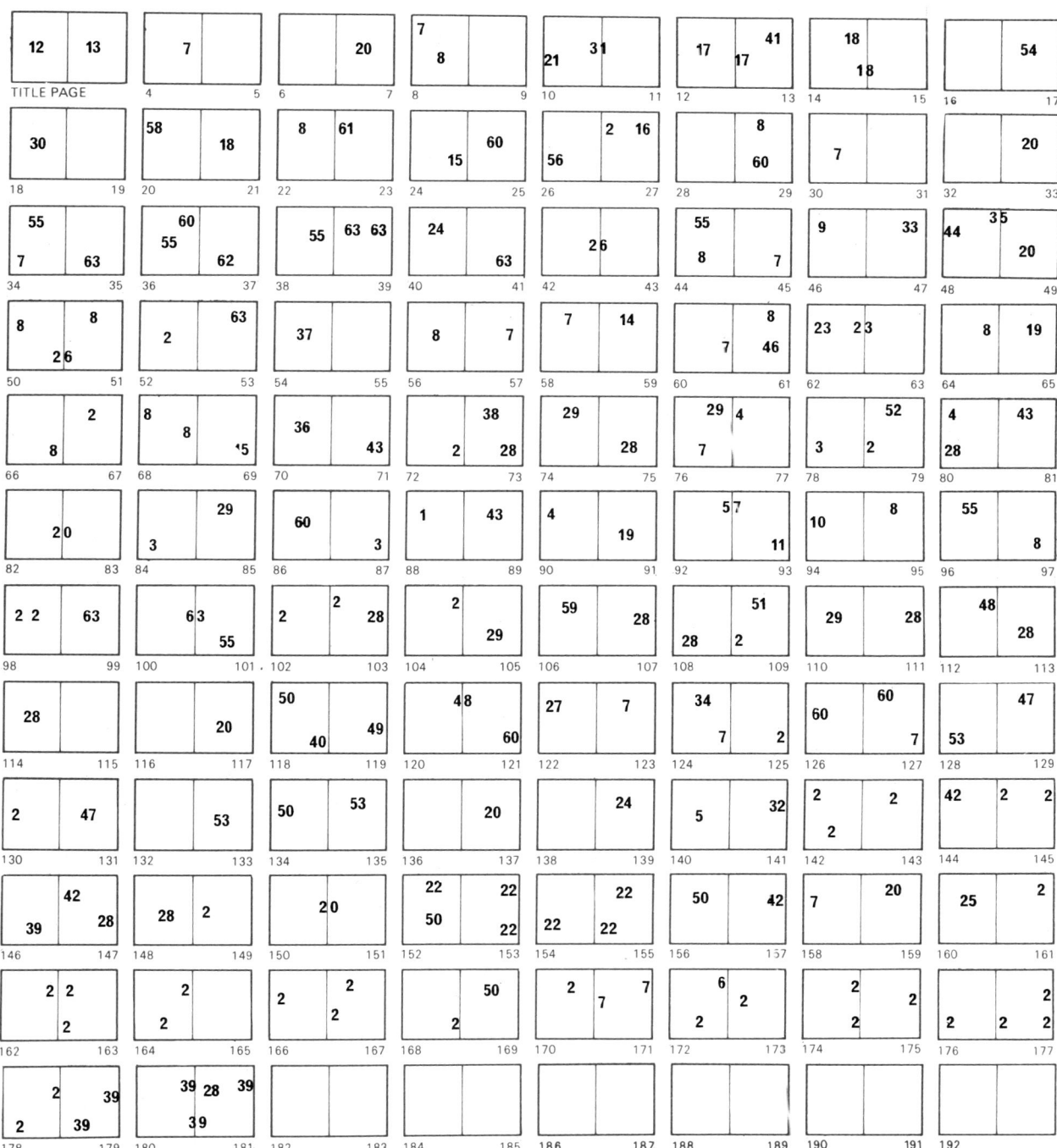